Sadhu Sundar Singh

Sadhu Sundar Singh
A Personal Memoir

by
Charles Freer Andrews

SCRIPTURE TESTIMONY EDITION

WALKING TOGETHER PRESS
ESTES PARK · JENTA MANGORO

© 2023 Walking Together Press

Published in 2023 by
Walking Together Press
Estes Park, Colorado USA
Jenta Mangoro, Jos, Plateau Nigeria
https://walkingtogether.press

ISBN: 978-1-961568-18-1

Originally published in 1934 by Harper & Brother Publishers, New York
Text from 1934 edition

Scripture Testimony Index content © 2023 Walking Together Press, all rights reserved

Cover design by D. Thaine Norris
Typeset in Adobe Garamond Pro by Lengdung Tungchamma and D. Thaine Norris

1

About the Scripture Testimony Edition

IN a time of profound personal crisis, in which his lifetime of intense spiritual devotion still offered no peace, Sundar Singh was defeated and determined to kill himself if he could not find the True God. Half an hour before the appointed time with the deadly train track, he had a vision of Jesus Christ, the one who saves. This encounter forever changed Sundar Singh and set him on the path of being a Christian *Sadhu,* or holy man, who—with "neither purse, nor scrip"—walked barefoot from village to village and over mountain passes to Tibet, preaching the Good News of Jesus Christ. Sadhu Sundar Singh's life of simple faith in—and total devotion to—his Master is a powerful demonstration of the reality of God and of the truth of His Word.

Data science reveals trends and patterns in information. The *Scripture Testimony Index* is an extensive research project using artificial intelligence and data science to develop a New-Testament-driven subject index across a large body of missionary biographies and personal narratives. As the story enthusiasts at Walking Together Press study these books programmatically; beautiful, bright threads emerge—threads of prayer, provision, deliverance, specific leading, healing, transformation, revival, and miraculous conversion. The end result is an index of thousands of short story excerpts organized by subject and Bible verse that empirically demonstrate the truth of the Scriptures, and which is freely available on our website at https://walkingtogether.life. Another result of this research was the discovery of dozens of great books that are long out of print and in danger of being forgotten. The *Scripture Testimony Collection* is a set of such books which we enthusiastically recommend, to the degree that we are making the effort to republish them.

Walking Together Press has enhanced this classic title, *Sadhu Sundar Singh,* by adding seventeen *Scripture Testimony* boxes in the text identifying Biblical topics and verses that are demonstrated by a specific portion of the narrative. An extensive *Scripture Testimony Index* has been added at the end containing short summaries of how each Scriptural topic is illustrated, making it easier to locate specific stories.

To
the Memory of My Friend
SUSIL KUMAR RUDRA

Contents

Preface

THE years, in Sadhu Sundar Singh's life, with which this memoir chiefly deals, were the greatest and the best. He had just come out victorious from an agonizing spiritual struggle, and had found in Christ the fulfilment of his soul's true desire. His enterprise to reach Tibet had called forth all his powers. The sacrifice, which such an effort demanded from him, had created in his inner spirit a radiant joy which shone out in every look and deed.

When I first knew him, he was at the height of early manhood and endowed with a splendid physique. His character, through the discipline of inward conflict, had been rendered resolute and strong. Body, mind and spirit were at last united in a single purpose. His sensitive imagination was alert to every sight and sound in Nature. Above and beyond all, he was devoted to his Saviour, who had fully claimed his service at the hour of his conversion. Thus he was ready joyfully to "endure hardness as a good soldier of Jesus Christ."

In the Spirit of Youth, a joyous confidence perpetually rises afresh which laughs at dangers and overcomes them. Death itself is looked full in the face and conquered. There is a great thought contained in a mystical poem of the eighteenth century on the nativity* which speaks of the birth of the Saviour:

---

* By Christopher Smart(1722-71)

xiii

"O the magnitude of meekness,
Worth from worth immortal sprung!
O the strength of infant weakness,
If eternal is so young!
If so young and thus eternal———"

How can we explain the deathless beauty in the heart of Youth except in terms of Him who is ever young, because He holds in His hands the keys of Death, and can say in triumph, "O Grave, where is thy victory?"

The personal reminiscence of the Sadhu which I have tried to give in the chapters which follow, has the great advantage of being able to concentrate on those stirring and eventful times when Sundar Singh was young. Afterwards, while middle age crept slowly forward, he was crippled by illness, and his youthful vigor departed. He struggled on and in the end was not defeated. That later period of his life will also come before us; but the days when I knew him best were the days of his youth.

II

Many centuries before Christ was born, the soul of the East had expressed in words of sadness mingled with longing its search for the living God.

The verses of the forty-second Psalm still move us with their beauty as we read them over to-day:

"Like as the hart desireth the waterbrooks, so panteth my soul after Thee, O God.

"My soul is athirst for God, yea, even for the Living God; when shall I come and appear before the presence of God?

"My tears have been my meat day and night; while they daily say unto me, Where is now thy God?

"Why art thou so heavy, O my soul? And why art thou so disquieted within me?

"O put thy trust in God, for I shall yet praise Him: who is the help of my countenance and my God."

India, perhaps, more than any other country in the world, has felt in her soul this thirst for the living God. No one, who has watched the long line of pilgrims on their way to some sacred shrine, can ever forget the mystery of this heart-longing to seek and to find God's presence. Age after age, the perpetual search goes on: the eternal quest is repeated. Sadhu Sundar Singh was in the great succession of those who had sought and found.

"The pearl-diver," sings a village mystic, "must dive to the bed of the ocean if he would win the pearl most precious."

Sundar was dedicated by his mother to the life of religion long before he was called and chosen to become a disciple of Christ. He brought over into his new Christian experience a devotion for the religious life which had been already fostered by a mother's love. He never disowned the spiritual heritage of the past. Rather, he was always deeply thankful for the truths about God which he had learnt in his early youth. He was like the merchant man in the Gospel parable, seeking goodly pearls, "who, when he had found one pearl of great price, went and sold all that he had and bought it."

The Sikh religion, which was his own ancestral faith, contained many goodly pearls; but his heart could not find its perfect rest until he had discovered, in Christ Himself, the One pearl of great price, and had sacrificed everything he held dear in His service.

The word "Sadhu," by which he became known both in the East and West, has a long Hindu tradition behind it. It implies one who has chosen for himself the life of a homeless wanderer in search of spiritual truth. Under the impulse of this ideal, men and women have left their kindred, and given up wealth and power, in order to go out in solitary faith on this lonely search for God. Even children, in India, have often been carried along by the same irresistible urge from within.

In the Sadhu's heart, when he had become a Christian, the devotion still remained; but it had reached a higher stage. For he could speak now with joy as one of those who had found peace. In every new trial of faith, he had Jesus, his Lord and Master, by his side, strengthening and upholding him. Thus, while he drank deeply of the cup of suffering, there was a spiritual power sustaining him which he had never known before.

During the years when I was nearest to him and saw him most frequently, his love for Christ was so ardent that at times it filled him with rapture. There was also to be noticed in him a singular gentleness of spirit. This was one of those "marks of the Lord Jesus" which had come to him through much suffering and humiliation.

He seemed to live consciously in the very presence of his Lord, and to carry that presence with him wherever he went. Men and women "took knowledge of him that he had been with Jesus." His inner joy sprang from the fountain of Life itself.

Those special years were full of crisis for the young Church in the North of India. The gravest issues concerning the future had been raised all over the Punjab. A struggle for spiritual liberty had begun, no less vital than that of the first age, when St. Paul claimed the full freedom of the Spirit on behalf of the Gentile Christians. Sundar Singh, by his creative personality, set forward a true type for Indian Christians to follow. He was thus continually in my thoughts and prayers both as a personal friend and also as the champion of a great cause.

III

In this memoir of the Sadhu, I have gone back continually to my own vivid remembrance of him during the time when we were like brothers together, inspired by one common devotion to our Lord and Master, Jesus Christ. The recollections of his personal friends, which have been gathered for this book, have also been used. Those who have helped me in this manner are far too numerous to mention by name; but I would ask them to accept my heartfelt thanks for the service they have rendered to the memory of one whom we all loved so well. An earnest desire has been recently expressed that a selection from the Sadhu's different writings should be published for future reference. They are likely to be of great value in the generations to come as revealing the original mind of an Indian Christian mystic in the early days of the Church in the Punjab.

Most generous help and encouragement have been rendered to me by the Rev. Arthur and Mrs. Parker, Drs. Streeter and Appasamy, and Dr. Heiler, who have already covered the whole ground of the Sadhu's life in the books which they have written. To these books I have constantly referred with very deep appreciation. With them, I would warmly thank at the same time Canon Chandu Lal and the Rev. T. E. Riddle, who are the Sadhu's trustees, for their deep sympathy with what I have undertaken and the help they have rendered to me.

My thanks are due to Messrs. Macmillan & Co., George Allen & Unwin, Ltd., Fleming H. Revell Co. and Cassell & Co., for the kind permission they have given me to quote from the Sadhu's writings.

A list of the Sadhu's books will be found at the end of the volume. Gertrude Newell has admirably done my typing.

This personal memoir had its beginning in India, in the midst of a circle of friends of the Sadhu, who had learnt to love him on account of his pure Christian devotion and wished to keep his memory fresh and green for the new Christian generation. Our united wish has been to seek to continue his work of love and service with the same spirit of sacrifice which he made manifest in all his actions. We look forward to the near future when the new spiritual life, which has come to the Christian Church in the West through the "Group" Movement, will touch also the hearts of those in the East who long for the coming of Christ's Kingdom. Our joy will be great if this record of the Sadhu is used to prepare the way for this renewal of the Spirit.

At the very time when these chapters were being completed the most terrible earthquake in present human experience occurred in the North of India, at the foot of the Himalayas, not far from the centre of Sadhu Sundar Singh's own labours. Thousands of human lives have been destroyed, and millions of those who have survived have suffered loss. This writing had to be laid aside in order to go about in England and elsewhere to make known the magnitude of the disaster and the extent of human misery involved. The bonds of sympathy between India and the world have been drawn closer by the common effort to relieve the sufferers. It is my hope, as far as possible, out of the funds which may come from the sale of this volume, to make a fitting contribution to the Earthquake Relief work, which is so nobly being carried on in North Behar.

The final revision and correction of this manuscript has been carried through in my new home, close to Woodbrooke, where a peaceful retreat has been provided for me by the kindness of friends.

C. F. ANDREWS.

25 FOX HILL, SELLY OAK,
   BIRMINGHAM.

SADHU SUNDAR SINGH

But God forbid that I should glory save in the cross of our Lord Jesus Christ, by whom the world is crucified unto me and I unto the world.

Galatians 6:14

Introduction

I

We had gone forward on our march beyond Simla, along the Hindustan-Tibet Road, into the interior, passing in and out among the nearer ranges of the Himalayas. Principal Rudra, with his two sons, Sudhir and Ajit, were my companions on the journey. The long vacation had arrived, just as the heat of the plains had become almost unbearable. We were now gloriously free from our college work in Delhi, and at leisure to wander far into the Hills which led towards Tibet.

Arrangements had already been made for our stay at Bareri, above Kotgarh, under the kindly care of Mrs. Bates, and we were eagerly looking forward to the warm welcome which she would give us at the end of our long march. Glimpses of the distant snows had startled us at different turning-points in the road by their marvelous beauty. The clear-cut mountain ridges standing out white against the deep blue sky seemed to beckon us onward.

The weather had been in our favour from the very start. A short break had come in the rains, and a spell of glorious sunshine had followed the first heavy deluge of the monsoon. Nature was offering us, with both hands, her lavish gifts. The high mountain air was cool and fragrant: every hill slope was covered afresh with its mantle of green grass. Butterflies hovered from flower to flower, and the singing of birds was with us as we walked along. When we reached Bareri at last, all the weariness, which we had felt before, had passed away, and our hearts were filled with a deep content.

II

Then, one day, we met Sadhu Sundar Singh. He was still quite young in age and youthful also in appearance. His wistful shyness had first to be overcome before he could be altogether at ease with us. For we were complete strangers to him and he had only recently become a Christian. During the time of transition from his old life to the new, he had met with many difficulties and some unexpected rebuffs. Therefore he was diffident and reserved until he came to know us intimately as his friends. Then his whole nature blossomed out in a singularly happy manner and he won our hearts by his gentle goodness.

His face had the look of childhood fresh upon it, in spite of marks of pain which were there also. At first sight, however, it was not so much his face that attracted my attention as his marvellous eyes. They were luminous, like the darkly gleaming water of some pool in the forest which a ray of sunlight has touched. While there was a shade of sorrow in them, there was also the light of joy and peace.

During the larger part of the time we were together, he seemed almost entirely to be absorbed in his own thoughts. But suddenly there would come into his eyes a flash of quick intelligence as he looked up and said a few words in reply to some question. The discipline of inner self-restraint was noticeable, and when he made a remark the effect was all the greater because of his previous silence.

In later years, the dignity of his presence deeply impressed me; but on that first occasion I seemed to see nothing but those eyes of his looking into my own and offering me his friendship. They seemed to tell me, without any formal words, how great a treasure his soul had found in Christ, and how he had realized at a glance that my heart was one with his own in devotion to the same Lord.

Principal Rudra began to tell in detail the story of our journey from Simla. He pictured, with happy laughter, the difficulties we had met at one stage of our march, when the whole of our bedding was left behind and we had to improvise, in the dak bungalow, some miscellaneous covering for the night. Sundar Singh's face lighted up with a smile, for the moment, as the story was told; but his active mind seemed to be far distant, as if he were out and away, in his own thoughts, traversing the lands beyond the snows.

That far-away look I have constantly witnessed since and have learnt to understand its meaning. For soon after he had received the open vision of his Lord, and was wholly converted to Christ's service, he surrendered his life to his Master to do with it what He desired. Then the command had come to him, with an irresistible compulsion of love, to go forward across the mountains into the Forbidden Land of Tibet in order to make known to the Tibetan people the unsearchable riches of Christ. Freely he had received, freely he must give.

This call from Christ had reached his heart, with such constraining power that it absorbed his waking thoughts and was present with him even in his dreams. Through all the years that were to come, it never left him; and everything points to his having laid down his life at last in order to obey it.

III

The road into Tibet, when it reaches Narkhanda, passes through a primeval forest, where the huge pine trees lift their heads high up into the sky. They stand like giant sentinels on the steep mountain-side waving their arms in the air. Out of the midst of these pine forests the road takes a sharp turn and descends to a point, not far from Bareri, where a second road leads down to Kotgarh. It was at Kotgarh that we met the Sadhu first, and its name will always be associated with his memory in my own mind because of that meeting. Year after year he started out from Kotgarh to reach the borders of Tibet.

This little hamlet, with its church in the centre, and its hospital and school, lies nestling far below the road to Tibet surrounded by forest. Open spaces have been kept for orchards and for fields of Indian corn. In those earlier days, an old, white-haired German missionary and his wife, named Mr. and Mrs. Beutel, used to live next to the church in the centre of the village. Another aged missionary, Dr. Jukes, came to live later on in a second bungalow, half-way up the hill, and ministered to the sick and dying for many miles around. The small hospital and dispensary, near to the church, were in his charge.

The Hindustan-Tibet Road above Kotgarh passes on for some miles at the higher level through open forest glades and patches of land under cultivation. It then descends rapidly, in a zigzag manner, until it drops right down to the sandy bed of the River Sutlej. From the higher part of the road, a remarkable view of the Sutlej is obtained as it winds to and fro, four thousand feet below, looking like a gleaming snake among the trees. When the river bed is reached at last, the heat in the valley, enclosed on every side by high mountains, is very great indeed.

Rampur, the capital of Bashahar State, lies farther on along the valley bed. At this point, Hindu India begins to disappear and Buddhist Central Asia seems to come slowly filtering in. Prayer-wheels and prayer-flags make their appearance everywhere on the landscape. The Mongolian features more and more predominate among the hill men and women who are met on the road. Each fresh sign indicates that the Hindu civilization is being left behind and a new area of human culture has begun.

Out of the river valley, beyond Rampur, the Hindustan-Tibet Road rises quite abruptly and reaches, by a very steep ascent, its higher levels once more. The traveller catches glimpses of the Sutlej, thousands of feet below, disappearing for a time and then coming back into sight as it winds its tortuous course amid the hills.

The road into Tibet soon becomes nothing more than a very difficult and often dangerous mountain track running along the higher
ledges. Although the actual frontier lies much farther on, the whole of
this section of the country belongs naturally by race and language to
the Tibetans, and might be called Lesser Tibet. It was only included
in India for strategic purposes when the Hindustan-Tibet Road was
first made.

IV

The story of martyrdom, in different centuries, suffered by those
who sought to make known the name of Jesus Christ in Tibet, is full
of heroic struggle against overwhelming odds. Different Franciscan
and monastic Orders of the Roman Catholic Church carried on the
great enterprise with a devotion that wins our highest admiration.

In the fourteenth century, a Franciscan Friar, named Odoric, first
entered the highlands of Tibet, and carried on his work amid incredible hardships.

His one devoted aim was to spread the message of the Gospel of
his Lord and Saviour Jesus Christ; but nothing of a permanent character was then accomplished.* Three centuries passed by, and in the
seventeenth century, the Portuguese Jesuit, Fra D'Andrada, lived and
laboured with the utmost fortitude in Tibet for many years. At a later
date, Desideri, by his scholarly writings, made a great impression. He
handed on his work to the Capuchin Fathers, who attempted in the
eighteenth century to found a more definitely organized mission. But
they too were obliged to give up an almost impossible task. Another
century passed away, and then high hopes were raised, in 1846, when
the Lazarists, Hue and Gabet, starting from Chinese territory, were
allowed to settle for a time in Lhasa, the capital. But again, amid much
persecution, the Tibetans who had become Christians were imprisoned
and the missionaries were driven out.

---

*   See notes, pp. 149f.

All these different enterprises were undertaken from the Chinese side of Asia. Other attempts were made by the intrepid Catholic missionaries to enter Tibet by way of India, along the valley of the Sutlej, even before the Hindustan-Tibet Road was built. These also ended in failure and Tibet still remained a forbidden land.

In more recent times, the Moravian missionaries from Herrnhut, representing the Reformed Churches of Europe, penetrated the mountain passes by way of Kotgarh to a place on the Sutlej called Poo-i. There a permanent mission station was built among a purely Tibetan population. They extended their work as far as the border. It would be impossible to speak too highly of the Christian endurance of this tiny band of missionaries in their pioneer work. For more than sixty years they persevered with undaunted courage. But after the war, financial difficulties became too great, and in 1925 they asked the Salvation Army to take over their mission stations. This has now been accomplished, and all those who have gone out from the Salvation Army have literally "counted not their lives unto the death." We, in our sheltered homes, can only dimly understand the dangers they are called upon to face.

When Dr. Sven Hedin, the renowned Swedish explorer, came down from the higher mountain passes of the interior, and reached at last the Hindustan-Tibet Road in 1909, the Moravians, at Poo-i, were the first to give him a welcome. His second resting-place, after some days' hard travelling on foot, was at Kotgarh, where he stayed at the mission house with Mr. Beutel before going forward to Simla.

At the time when Dr. Sven Hedin arrived, I was staying at Bareri, nursing an Indian Christian student who was ill with rheumatic fever and in great pain. My first sight of the great traveller was in the little mission church on one Sunday evening, when I noticed a bearded stranger in front of me listening very attentively to the service. When I collected the offertory, after the sermon, he signed his name, "Sven Hedin," on a piece of paper, instead of putting in a coin. Thus I knew for certain that he had come, and eagerly greeted him after the service was over. We sat up very late that night, while he showed me on his maps the new discoveries he had made among the highest mountain ranges of the Himalayas. Before the evening had ended, he presented his gold chronometer, which had been of such help to him on his journey, to the Kotgarh Christian Mission as a thank-offering to God for all the mercies he had received.

Before he left us, I asked him if he would be able to visit Amar Nath, the Indian student, who was so ill at Bareri. He very gladly consented to do so, and stayed talking with him for over an hour, while the boy's eyes glowed with pleasure and excitement.

Up and down this long road into Tibet, Sadhu Sundar Singh used to make his way on foot, year after year, with never-failing courage. He frequently journeyed alone and he was well known to the Moravian missionaries at Poo-i, who always looked forward to his coming. During the winter months the mountain passes are blocked with snow and ice, but as soon as they were open in the springtime, he would make this journey. To be able to endure, as a Sadhu, the severe hardships he encountered in every kind of weather, required great physical stamina and powers of endurance. There were also dangers of different kinds to be met with on the way and any accident might prove fatal for want of medical aid. It may possibly have happened that in this very region, among the mountains, some final disaster overtook him.

Even now it is strangely difficult for those who knew him best to think of him as dead. Last year, when I went to Simla in order to obtain all the available information about him from those who had deeply loved him, there was always a questioning note and hesitation when speaking of him as dead, as though after all he might even then be alive. In spite of the Government of India's notice, which accepted his death as certain (after a period of more than four years' searching inquiry), there were many who still regarded it as doubtful, thinking that he might have retired into solitude for a longer period than usual, and that he would some day reappear.

The ultimate problem of his fate will be considered at the end of this volume. But the very fact that so many of those who knew him refuse to believe that he is dead, is itself a significant thing. It tells its own story. For Sundar Singh had received from Jesus Christ, deep in his own inner life, an immortal spring of youth, a fountain of living water. His greatest deeds of heroism, by which he was remembered, held within them the true secret of

"the wondrous Cross
Where the young Prince of Glory died." *

Therefore those who loved him most of all could hardly believe that he had passed away.

SCRIPTURE TESTIMONY
The sheep know and hear His voice
JOHN 10:3-4 · JOHN 10:16
Holy Spirit directs believers in ministry
MATTHEW 10:19-20 · ACTS 8:29 · ACTS 13:2 · ACTS 15:28 · ACTS 16:6-10 · ACTS 20:22 · ROMANS 8:14

A slight incident at Kotgarh, when we were with him, may be given as an illustration; for it reveals the source of that inner life which was "hid with Christ in God."

He got up one night from prayer and was preparing to go out alone. When questioned why he was starting out so late at night, he replied that he had heard the call of someone from the valley below who was needing his immediate help. Those who were sleeping by his side implored him to wait until the early dawn and not to risk the dangers of the forest throughout the night. But the Sadhu insisted on starting at that very moment. After a few days' absence, he returned. The person he had gone to seek had been very seriously ill and had greatly needed his assistance.

---

* This is the original form of the great hymn.

This sudden call by the Spirit within him, communing with his own spirit during a night of silent prayer, was in keeping with Sundar Singh's whole life as a Christian; and his immediate obedience without fear was of the same character. Such things as these illuminate with a fullness of new meaning the great words of the Apostle: "For as many as are led by the Spirit of God, they are the sons of God."

Another scene at the Lepers' Home at Chandkuri may complete the picture of his Christ-likeness. The joy of the lepers, we read, was overflowing when they listened to the Sadhu telling them of the love of God. He went to each one who was

SCRIPTURE TESTIMONY
It is the heart of Jesus to show compassion to the needy
MATTHEW 9:36 · MATTHEW 14:13-21 · MARK 1:41 · MARK 6:34 · LUKE 7:13

sick in turn and spoke some words of comfort. Especially he stayed for a long time in the children's room, and showed his love for them in every tender look he gave them. His farewell words were a message of peace. He prayed for them all with earnestness the great prayer: "May the peace of God which passeth all understanding keep your hearts and minds in the knowledge and love of God and of His Son Jesus Christ," and there were tears in many eyes as they bade him "Good-bye."

V

As he parted from them to go forward on his perilous journey across the mountains into Tibet, he asked for their prayers and blessings in return? and so he passed on his way to meet the difficulties of the journey, rejoicing most of all to suffer for Christ's sake.

What was Sadhu Sundar Singh like to look upon in his Eastern dress? How did he impress people by his appearance when they first met him?

These and similar questions have been put to me many times over by those who never had any opportunity of seeing him in person, but yet have been deeply moved by his romantic life and his steadfast Christian faith.

The simplest way to answer such questions is to turn to the frontis-piece of this memoir, where the Sadhu is seen standing in the grounds of Kingsmead, Selly Oak, Birmingham, during his first visit to the West in the year 1919. This full-length portrait is the best which I have been able to obtain of him, and it is one of the very few that really do him justice. It was taken while he was the guest of the Warden of Kingsmead, J. W. Hoyland, to whom he became deeply attached. Soon after he had arrived in England, he stayed for a time in the Selly Oak Colleges, and his visit made such a deep impression on the staff and students that it is vividly remembered even up to the present day. I have records with me of this visit which show clearly the unique effect it had upon those who saw and heard him. The same record has been given me from other centres also. All this evidence goes to prove that there was something indefinable about his personality which arrested immediate attention.

Sundar Singh belonged by birth to the Sikhs of the Punjab. Among the different peoples of the world, the Sikhs, with their military tradi-tion, possess a physique which can hardly be surpassed. Sundar's own stature, when he was young, was quite up to the standard of his race. He stood slightly over six feet in height when he had come to his full manhood.

Though he ceased, after becoming a Christian, to wear the long hair of the Sikhs, he continued all through his life to retain the full beard, which is one of the marked characteristics prescribed by the Sikh religion. Indeed, as a Christian, he made very little change in his outward dress and habits, all the while living as a Sadhu. He wished to remain one at heart with his own people, and also in his outward appearance. In this he set an example to other Indian Christians; and many in consequence to-day are laying aside their European dress and giving up their European surnames, in order to draw nearer to their own countrymen.

Even when travelling in Europe and America and the Far East, he did not alter to any extent his outward dress; and it was most difficult for his friends to persuade him to wear even a cloak over his Indian robe as a protection against the damp cold of the North.

He was rightly very proud of his noble tradition as a Sikh. Therefore, when he became a Christian, he wished to preserve all the good he had received from his own upbringing, and not to allow it to perish. For he believed, with an ever-increasing conviction, that the religious teaching which he had obtained as a child at his mother's knee was noble and good. He remembered the words of Jesus, his Master, concerning the Jewish faith, when He said: "Think not that I am come to destroy the law or the prophets: I am not come to destroy, but to fulfil."

Holding himself magnificently erect, with a perfectly natural poise, he looked the very picture of young manhood, such as some great master-painter or sculptor might have taken for his model. There was a singular refinement in his features which softened away any hard lines that might have betokened mere physical force. Though he came from a fighting race, the combative spirit died down in him even as a child; for from the first he was wholly devoted to religion.

From his boyhood onwards he had been rather a sufferer than a fighter; and when I knew him best, during his youthful days, the marks of that inner suffering of the soul were still visible upon him. His eyes, which had so strangely drawn me towards him, showed signs that their deep, inner peace had only been attained after much conflict. He had gained a haven of rest, not without anguish; for the Cross, which his Master carried, was never far away from the disciple; yet he had learned at length to bear it lightly as the easy yoke of Christ.

One thing I noticed most of all during those years when my intercourse with him was most frequent and our friendship in Christ most intimate: whenever the name of the Master, whom he loved and served, was mentioned, his whole face became lighted up with a joyous brightness and radiance. From the day when he had seen the Heavenly Vision, there had been only one passionate interest in his active life—to take up his cross and follow Christ his Lord.

His whole appearance was modified greatly by his ill-health in later years. The very heavy strain he had put upon his heart, in earlier days, had seriously weakened his physique, and his journeys to different parts of the world had added to the injury which had thus been started. At last he could only with difficulty move about from place to place in the Hills. The necessary exertion of going up-hill made him pant for breath and caused him pain. Gradually this induced a heaviness of body, owing to his inability to continue the active life which he had always led in the past. But though his outward appearance was thus altered, his inner life seemed to become more humble and gentle than ever as it drew towards its close. He longed for death, and we may believe that his longing has at last been fulfilled.

VI

After his return from Europe it became impossible for me to meet him as often as I wished, for my own duties in the Ashram* at Santiniketan kept me in Bengal, while he lived far away in the North among the Simla Hills. Besides this, I was obliged again and again to go abroad in order to visit Indians overseas; and he himself went abroad also, but in a different direction.

But on one well-remembered occasion at Whitsuntide, in the year 1926, we met together at St. Thomas's Church, Simla, just below die Mall, when our mutual friend, Canon Chandu Lal, was also present with us. Sundar Singh had looked forward to this meeting and had come into Simla especially for that purpose. It was a rare opportunity for both of us, and we were able to spend the whole afternoon together, speaking about the things of Christ and His Kingdom that were dearest to our hearts. When the farewell moment came, a very strong impression was left upon my mind that we might never see each other again in this world.

---

*   A place of religious retreat.

During that last meeting, as we conversed together, I noticed at once the marked physical change which had come over him. His face was strangely altered from the clear-cut features I had known of old. He had aged very rapidly indeed. Some internal disease seemed already to have obtained its fatal hold and undermined his constitution, making an obvious difference even in his outward appearance.

This change alarmed and even shocked me, and I spoke to him with deep sympathy about it. He told me what he knew concerning his heart-trouble, which had developed after his tour in the West. Also I learnt about other serious illnesses from which he had suffered. On one occasion, in Calcutta, he was nursed back to health only with the greatest difficulty. How far the heart disease had then advanced, it is difficult to say. But at this final farewell, when he bade me good-bye in Simla, he appeared to me like a man who was already looking death in the face.

All through our conversation together, there was a drawn, pained expression while he spoke—as if suffering was very near the surface. Now and again he showed me, by some involuntary movement, the bodily pain which could not be hidden. He would turn aside for a moment and then resume the conversation. It was possible in sympathy to understand the heavy burden he was carrying alone.

Perhaps, on this special afternoon, he was suffering more than he usually did. But, however that may be, it was impossible not to be gravely anxious about him when I saw him in this state. On making inquiries from him, I found out that though at intervals he was entirely free from pain, he never could be quite certain of his health, because his illness was likely to return.

In all his intercourse and communion with me at that time, he was the same loved friend and brother I had known of old. He had been quite unspoiled by the world's praise and had gone back into retirement with an evident sense of relief. Humble, devoted, obedient, he sought to follow his Lord and Master, Jesus Christ, and to refer every act of his life to His guidance. It was a great joy to me to note that he had not lost the happy gift of laughter which had always kept him childlike at heart. But though he said little about it, he was undoubtedly very ill in body, and it was this that troubled me most of all.

After the first words of greeting, he spoke to me with intense earnestness about Christ and the coming of His Kingdom. From this supreme subject his thoughts hardly ever seemed to wander. The ardent desire to start once more on the long journey into Tibet was still uppermost with him. His eager spirit was ever seeking that Hindustan-Tibet Road, but his bodily weakness seemed to make such an effort quite out of the question.

Whether my surmise at the time was correct or no, I cannot tell, but instinctively I felt that he was longing for his Master's command, which should bid him lay down his heavy burden and leave the struggle for those that should come after. He desired, with a very deep longing, "to depart and be with Christ which is far better."

Long ago, in the early dawn of youth, he had heard the Master's word: "Follow thou me," and he had left all to follow Jesus. He had been eager to die for His sake. Now he seemed rather to be "tarrying" till the Lord came.

How that word of the Lord had reached him in the early years of his life, and how he had faithfully obeyed, this book will seek to explain.

Chapter I

Early Days

THE old ancestral home in the North Punjab, where Sundar Singh was born, was at Rampur, a Sikh village in the Patiala State. His father, Sardar Sher Singh, was a man of considerable wealth, who was looked upon as their ruling chief by the villagers round about. Sundar's early years were therefore passed in comfort as compared with the hard lot of the agricultural labourers who tilled the soil. Certain of the senior members of the family held rank under the Maharajah, in the service of the Patiala State, and one of them had gained distinction.

The domestic life that was lived each day in the Sardar's home by Sundar and his brothers was almost untouched by the modern civilization from the West which had been introduced by the British Raj. The ancient household traditions and old religious observances were carried on throughout the year without any break. The English language was hardly ever spoken. There was a noble dignity about this old Sikh life, in an Indian state, which the twentieth century has somewhat rudely disturbed. At the same time, much that was corrupt and decayed was allowed to remain unremoved.

The ancient personal authority of the Maharajah of Patiala continued to be exercised in full without any check on his arbitrary rule.

Society was built up on an aristocratic basis with the Maharajah himself as its supreme ruler and chief, whose word was law. At the same time, the Sikh religion, which had always been recognized by the State, afforded to the humblest of its members a spiritual basis of equality, by establishing a religious brotherhood, called the Khalsa. While, as a Sardar, Sher Singh would be of superior rank to the villagers around him and they would fully recognize that superiority, yet as Sikhs they would be his spiritual equals.

For the Sikh religion, which has its home and centre in the Punjab, has always carried with it this note of equal brotherhood, wherein all men and women who profess the faith are regarded as one family in the sight of God. The divine is represented on earth by the Guru, or religious leader and teacher. But under the spiritual direction of the Guru all are united in one religious household of the Faith, wherein there is no rank or class or caste. It was this "brotherhood" ideal which gave the Sikhs such strength and cohesion, in their struggle for personal freedom, during the years of suffering and martyrdom when they revolted against the Moghul Emperor's rule.

It was not possible for me to visit the village of Rampur where Sundar Singh was born. Nevertheless, it is easy to picture the life led in such a home, because I have often been the guest of the Sikh villagers in the Punjab and shared their kindly hospitality. Still further, those enterprising Sikhs, who have gone abroad to Hong Kong, Fiji, British Columbia and elsewhere, have given me the warmest welcome, as a friend, and admitted me into their own house of worship*. For they have come to look upon me as an old and tried companion, and a willing and ready helper in any time of trouble. Therefore I can write personally, with full appreciation, concerning the all-important part which the Sikh religion plays in their lives, moulding their characters.

Often I have witnessed how the mother of the family in each Sikh household holds the place of honour among them. She comes first also in her children's affection. For one of the finest aspects of the

---

*   Called Gurdwira

Sikh religious life is the honour paid to woman and the high ideal of marriage that has accompanied it. The daily worship of the One Supreme God is carried on in the family by husband and wife. It is the first duty of every Sikh, both man and woman alike, to recite daily the verses of the sacred Scriptures in praise of the Supreme.

Some of my happiest days in India have been spent among the Sikhs, dwelling with them in their own homes, listening to their devotional songs, and sharing their life in common with them. I can say with conviction that the sacred words of their Gurus, repeated by their lips, have sunk deeply into their hearts. It would be difficult to find a more generous or forgiving people.

In village India, the age and date of birth of children is not recorded with any exactness; but it would appear likely that Sundar himself was born on September 3rd, 1889. He was the youngest son of Sardar Sher Singh. There were two elder brothers and one sister.

The whole joint family, of which Sardar Sher Singh was the head, would comprise his brothers with their children as well as his own household. All the children would live together in the one family house at Rampur. The cousins of Sundar Singh, when he was young, would be almost as near and dear to him as his own brothers. They would share everything together, as families do in India.

There is one distinguishing feature of the Sikh religion which gives it a character of its own. It was born out of persecution and suffering, and has always carried the mark of sacrifice, and even of martyrdom for the faith, written in large characters upon it. When this distinguishing mark of suffering has been prominent, the Sikh religion has flourished; when ease and compromise have taken its place, the Sikh religion has declined. Tertullian once said of the early Christians that the blood of the martyrs was the seed of the Church. This might also be truly stated concerning the religion of the Sikhs. We shall see, as this story proceeds, that just as Sundar Singh, when he became a Christian, took over into his new experience the Sadhu ideal, so also he held fast to the Sikh idea of martyrdom for the faith as the highest aspiration of mankind. For this central thought coloured the whole of his Christian life.

The mother of Sundar Singh was in every respect a remarkable woman. She was noted among those of her own household for her deep religious devotion and her innate purity of character. Nature had endowed her with great gifts of tender refinement and homely wisdom. She was singularly broadminded in her outlook upon the religious life, paying reverence to spiritual leaders among Sikhs and Hindus alike. When the Christian ladies of the American Mission came near to her village she was eager to receive visits from them.

We find from references in Sundar Singh's addresses in Ceylon, that his only sister inherited from her mother the same earnest devotion to religion which he had himself. This drew them close together when they were children, but she did not herself become a Christian. She remained a devout member of her own ancestral faith. "My sister," he said, "woke each morning at early dawn to perform her devotions and to keep her religious observances." With sad irony, he compares her to others in Christian homes, "who spend five minutes, and then are tired, but who hope to spend all eternity in praising God."

Sundar Singh was his mother's youngest and dearest child. He remained constantly by her side all through his earlier years. She exercised by far the greatest influence upon his character, and moulded more than anyone else his religious faith. When he was in Europe, Sundar would very often refer to her as the one who taught him most about God.

Long hours were given up to prayer each day by this devoted mother, with her young children as her constant companions. Whatever else might be laid aside, these duties of religion were never neglected. While performing her devotions, she visited in turn the Hindu temples and the Sikh shrines. Thus her whole life was surrounded by the atmosphere of religion.

Rising early, long before the dawn, she would take her ceremonial bath and then carry her flower-offering to the Hindu temple. Each daily act would be dedicated in some special way to God. At the end of the day she would once more make her offering of prayer and worship before retiring to rest. On different religious occasions she would listen, far into the night, while the sacred Scriptures were being recited. On certain days she would go without food in order that her prayers might be more earnest and acceptable to God. All her heart was poured out in devotion through ch channels as these; and her youngest son would be with her during her times of prayer and worship, watching and imitating his mother, as a child will often do.

Her other sons had not been able to follow the strict religious life which she had endeavoured to teach them. This only made her all the more earnest in her daily prayers, and she longed to dedicate, from the very first, her youngest son entirely to God, as the one treasure she had left.

"You must seek peace in your own soul," she said to him, "and love religion; and then some day you will become a holy Sadhu."

Already she had taken him with her from time to time into the forest, where an aged, white-bearded Sadhu dwelt. She used to seek out this old saint, in order to get counsel and advice from him in the things of the Spirit. She could imagine no greater or nobler destiny for her younger son than this, that he should become a man of God, like this saintly old man who was her own preceptor.

As we read some of her words, related to us by her son, we can easily picture to ourselves this Sikh mother with her youngest child. We can also realize the powerful effect which her influence would have upon his highly imaginative nature.

"It was the Holy Spirit," he tells us, "who made me a Christian; but it was my mother who made me a Sadhu."

The character of the father of Sundar Singh is most vividly brought before us in a story about him which his son tells at length in his last book, *With and Without Christ.* This book is in many ways the most self-revealing of all the Sadhu's writings, and reference will constantly be made to it on that account.

The story tells how his mother, from his very earliest years, had impressed upon him that if he wished to grow up with a desire to love God with all his heart he must abstain from every kind of sin, and also be full of sympathy and help to those in trouble. She herself was an example to him; for every day she used to perform her first religious duty of helping some poor person in need.

One day Sundar ran off to the bazaar to spend on some sweetmeats the pocket-money which his father had given to him. On the way he saw an old woman, famished with cold and hunger, while he had every comfort. "When she begged for some help from Sundar he gave her all the money he had; but the thought of her misery in the bitter cold haunted him as he went back.

Therefore, when he reached home, he ran to his father and told him all about it, saying impulsively that unless she was given a blanket she would surely die of cold. His father put him off, saying that he had often helped her before, and now it was someone else's turn to assist her in her need.

But this did not satisfy the impetuous boy in the least, and when all his entreaties were in vain, he stole five rupees belonging to his father and rushed back to the beggar-woman intending to give the money to her for a blanket. But his conscience pricked him on the way, and without giving her the money he returned to the house, miserable at heart, and hid the five rupees. Very soon his father missed the stolen money and asked Sundar whether he had taken it.

The young boy denied it, telling a lie on the spur of the moment. His father at once believed him for Sundar had always been a truthful lad. But though he had been able to escape from punishment by thus telling a falsehood, his conscience tormented him so much all through the night that he could not sleep. Early in the morning he went to his father and confessed both his theft of the money and the lie which he had told about it. He then gave back the five rupees.

He tells us how, by this act of confession, the burden of anguish was at once removed. The relief was so great that he was ready joyfully to bear whatever punishment his father might decide to inflict on him for his wrongdoing. But instead of punishing him, his father took the young lad in his arms and said, with tears in his eyes: "I have always trusted you, my child, and now I have good proof that I was not wrong!"

The father then gave to his son the joy of helping the poor woman and all was forgiven. The deep affection which the young boy had for his father, after that act of tender forgiveness, was hardly less than the love he gave to his mother, who was all in all to him in those childhood days.

Perhaps the greatest suffering that Sundar Singh had to endure in later years was when he was obliged to tell his father that he must put even his love in the second place as a Christian, in order faithfully to follow Christ. We may well believe, also, that the greatest joy that ever came into his life was when his father, at the very end of his days, confessed his heart allegiance to Christ and became His true disciple.

Chapter II

The Search for God

SUNDAR Singh's early childhood, as he grew up under his mother's care in the family home at Rampur, became more and more absorbed in the things of religion. His one desire was to find God. He had learnt from his mother that there was a peace of soul which was the greatest treasure that anyone could possess. Therefore he sought it with all his heart.

Everywhere in his writings, when he speaks of his childhood, he tells us about the intensity of this search, and how it occupied all his thoughts. While other boys were at their games, he was seeking to find out the meaning of religious texts. When he was seven years old, he tells us, he had learnt the Gita* by heart. It is not unusual in India to find such precocity in childhood. We may therefore accept without hesitation his own story of these inner struggles which were so real to him even as a child.

"Often," he relates, "I used to read the Hindu Scriptures till midnight, in order that I might in some way quench the thirst of my soul for peace. My father objected, saying: 'It is bad for your health to read so

---

* The most famous Hindu scripture, admirably translated by Sir Edwin Arnold in a poem called "The Song Celestial."

late.' Though there was much in my home to make me happy, I was not attracted by it. My father often remonstrated with me, saying: 'Boys of your age think of nothing but games and play, but how has this religious mania possessed you at so early an age? There is plenty of time to think of these things later in life. I suppose you must have got this madness from your mother and the Sadhu.'"

The Sadhu here mentioned by Sundar's father was the aged teacher whom his mother used to consult on spiritual things. Greatly puzzled and bewildered, the old man did his utmost to satisfy the hunger and thirst for spiritual truth in this extraordinary child. But in the end he could only give him the kindly counsel of delay: "My child," he would say, "it is useless for you to waste time on these things now. The day will come when you yourself will understand them."

Such an answer, however, could not bring relief and so the deep longing continued and the inner struggle remained unresolved.

Thus the boy was not only a puzzle to his father, but also to his spiritual preceptors. There was only one person who could understand him and that was his mother. She had the instinct, deep down in her inner nature, which made her unerringly feel what suffering her child was going through, and she prayed for him night and day. To her the chief responsibility for his spiritual development was naturally entrusted, and she kept him always close by her side.

"I believe," said Sundar Singh, "that every religious man has a religious mother."

This wide generalization was made from his own personal experience, and it was not far from the truth. With him, as with most men and women of very deep convictions, the foundations of his spiritual faith were laid in childhood, and were due most of all to a mother's faith and prayer. No basis of life remains so strong as this in after years, and none is more secure.

"My mother," he wrote, "brought me up in a religious atmosphere. She prepared me for the work of God.... Whenever I think of her, I thank God for such a mother. She had a wonderful amount of Light.

I have seen many Christian women, but none of them came up to my mother."

Those who know India well and have lived longest among its people, have frequently met with examples of this close relationship in spiritual things between a mother and her child. Often in the Indian villages, where the religious life is quite natural and simple, these intimate human relationships go very deep indeed. Each day is uncrowded and the normal pace of life is never hurried. Therefore it is possible, here and there, for a mother, who is naturally devout, to become entirely absorbed in the things of religion, and to impart this instinct to her child. She is able, also, to remain in the midst of household affairs, and yet to continue her religious duties. With such a person, the greater portion of the common daily life takes a spiritual turn. The neighbours who live round about in the village accept this as a sign from God, and they allow an area of freedom, in such cases, which is a mark of silent appreciation.

Those who become thus wholly absorbed in God are called Bhaktas (devotees), and when that name has once been given to them, by popular consent, they are released from many of the ordinary duties of life, even while they still remain in Hindu society. Very gradually and almost imperceptibly, each part of the daily round, which does not come within the scope of their religious devotion, is given up. The other members of the home willingly accept this as a matter of course. The whole neighbourhood recognizes that the divine call has come which must be obeyed.

In certain cases, the Bhakta finally abandons all social ties whatsoever and becomes a Sannyasin.* In other instances, some minor duties within the home still continue, but the daily life even then becomes almost monastic in its solitary character—forming a cycle of incessant prayer and worship. Such Bhaktas carry on the age-long religious tradition of India. They are to be found, in every country district, throughout the length and breadth of the land.

---

* Ascetic

Sundar Singh's mother was true to this great Hindu ideal, and she carried her child along with her while she performed her religious duties. As he grew older, every thought of his mother's heart became more and more concentrated on his future. She longed for him to be a Sadhu. Her prayers were incessant and he understood their purpose. His intense love for his mother, which shows itself in every word he writes about her, made him all the more ready to respond to her dearest hopes.

When Sundar Singh was in the West, people noticed the constant allusions to his mother in his simple addresses. The beautiful picture he drew of her went home to everyone's heart, and his audiences thus became better able to understand the Sadhu himself.

"My mother," he wrote in one of his most revealing and inspiring books,* "used to rise daily before daylight, and after bathing would read the Gita and other Hindu Scriptures. I was influenced more than the rest of the family by her pure life and teaching. She early impressed on me the rule that my first duty on rising in the morning was that I should pray to God for spiritual food and blessing, and that only after so doing I should break my fast. At times I insisted that I should have food first; but my Godfearing mother, sometimes with love and sometimes with punishment, fixed this habit firmly in my mind, that I should first seek God and afterwards other things. Although, at that time, I was too young to appreciate the value of those things, yet later on I realized their value; and now, whenever I think of it, I thank God for that training, and I can never be sufficiently thankful to God for giving me such a mother, who in my earliest years instilled in me the love and fear of God."

To a certain minister of religion in the West, who had made the suggestion to Sundar Singh that it might be well for him to spend some time in taking a course of theology at a Divinity School, he replied: "I have been to the best theological college in the world—my mother's bosom."

---

* *With or Without Christ*, p. 105f. published by Harper and Brother, New York.

On another occasion, in answer to a pious fundamentalist, who had assumed that because the Sadhu's mother was a Hindu and had not become a Christian, he would not meet her in heaven, he exclaimed: "If I do not see my mother in heaven, I shall ask God to send me to hell, in order that I may be with her there."

In both these answers we can feel his devoted love for his mother expressed with singular force and directness. They bring us to the heart of truth. Like all great sayings, which are simple and yet profound, they are not easily forgotten. For he would never for one moment allow any gulf to be made between his mother and himself; neither would he separate either Hinduism or the Sikh religion by hard and fast lines from the Christian Faith. They were woven out of one texture by the Divine Spirit, and they needed to be interwoven again into one perfect fabric.

"Christianity," he said to Canon Streeter, "is the fulfilment of Hinduism. Hinduism has been digging channels. Christ is the water to flow through these channels.... The Hindus have received of the Holy Spirit. There are many beautiful things in Hinduism; but the fullest light is from Christ."

"Everyone is breathing the air," he added, "so everyone, Christian or non-Christian, is breathing the Holy Spirit, though they do not call it by that name. The Holy Spirit is not the property of some special people."

The last sentence here quoted is wholly in accordance with Christ's teaching, and Sundar Singh had his mother's example before him to make him feel its truth.

"People call us 'heathen'!" he exclaimed, when conversing with the Archbishop of Upsala. "Just fancy! My mother a 'heathen'! If she were alive now, she would certainly be a Christian. But even while she followed her ancestral faith, she was so religious that the term 'heathen' makes me smile! She prayed to God, she served God, she loved God, far more warmly and deeply than many Christians. So far as I can see, there are many more people among us in India who

lead a spiritual life than there are in the West, although they do not
know or confess Christ.

"The 'heathen' in my country," he continued, "seek for God, not
during days or months only; they go on seeking earnestly and anxiously
to find the truth for years at a time; and during this search they have
to suffer many things.... But you—you Christians in the West—why!
you get tired in ten minutes! Yet nominal Christians, in these countries,
call the people in non-Christian lands 'heathen'!"

Few subjects aroused his moral indignation more in later years than
any insult to the sacred memory of his mother; and he repudiated the
doctrine which lay behind it with all his might.*

In keeping with this higher Christian truth he would assert that the
Holy Spirit is given to simple and humble souls of every faith. God
was no "respecter of persons," but in every community right living and
God-fearing people were accepted by Him. He would refer to his own
mother as a proof of this, and would declare with deep emotion that
she alone by her prayers, when he was a child, had kept his own heart
near to God. She had thus, however unconsciously, been God's chosen
instrument in leading him at last to Christ. If she had lived longer,
he fully believed that she would have come to the full knowledge of
Christ in joyful company with himself. Never for a moment could he
separate her in his thoughts from the love of Christ. That love would
have been altogether incomplete, if it had not included his mother in
its all-embracing fullness.

Thus Sundar Singh, like the child Samuel in the Old Testament, who
became a prophet, was literally the offspring of his mother's prayers.
Even at his mother's breast he was being reared, all unconsciously, for
God's service.

One of the greatest of the saints, Augustine, with his mother Monica,
might be given as another example of the power of a mother's love.
For in his Confessions he shows us clearly that he owed everything
to his mother, whose prayers and tears won him at last for Christ's

---

* See Notes, p. 151.

service. While other helpers, in Sardar Sher Singh's large household, gave a definite religious bent to the young child's mind, there was no one whose spiritual influence came near to that of his own mother.

The Sikh religion, with its daily devotions, gave him continual support in his childhood. We can trace out which of the verses in the Sikh Scriptures, chanted by his mother, would impress him most of all as a child; for we know how he still remembered them and repeated them after he had become a Christian.

"I cannot live," says Guru Nanak, "for a moment without Thee, my Lord. When I have Thee, I have everything. For Thou, O Lord, art my treasure." In the same strain, Guru Arjun continues: "We long for Thee, O Lord; we thirst for Thee. Only in Thee does our heart find rest." In another place, the noblest spiritual note is struck in these great words of the Granth Sahib:*

"Farid, if a man beat thee, strike him not in return, but stoop and kiss his feet."

"Farid, if thy soul hath longing for the Lord, become as grass for men to tread on."

"Farid, when one man breaketh thee, and another trampleth on thee, then thou enterest truly the Temple of God."

Out of such thoughts as these, which often remind us of the Sermon on the Mount, Sundar Singh each day found sustenance. But he tells us that in spite of all the wealth of spiritual truth thus set before him, he could not find satisfaction for the deepest longing of his soul. Sometimes the peace which he so ardently desired seemed at last about to be realized to the full; but then again it faded away and his heart became restless once more.

During these critical years, as he grew older, he spent long hours, under the instruction of different teachers, in those forms of Hindu mental and physical culture which are called Yoga. These comprise a series of movements and pauses, related to the body and mind, having a spiritual purpose in view. The object is to retain a rhythm

---

*   The name of the Sacred Scripture of the Sikh religion.

and concentration, and out of these a stillness. By starting a rhythm in deep breathing and by intense concentration the attempt is made to keep away every disturbing influence and thus to reach equilibrium and repose. The outward body and the conscious mind may be rendered quiescent in this manner, while the subconscious mind becomes actively awake.*

In India, the art of Yoga has been constantly practiced by Hindu men of religion. Some moderns believe that this art can actually be reduced to a science. There are those in the West who have taken it up as an idle pursuit and have thereby done themselves more harm than good. For the danger of self-hypnotism is always near at hand.

The young lad pursued this course of Yoga with the same intensity that he employed in other directions connected with religion. He was able at last by these means to throw himself into a trance, and do other psychical feats which he had seen the Yogis perform. But he tells us that although, for a time, his inner spirit seemed to be made calm by these means, and the things of the outer world vanished from him, the effect was only transitory. There was no abiding peace, or full inner realization.

"I wanted to save myself," he cries out with pathos. "How I studied all our sacred books! How I strove for peace and rest of soul! I did good works: I did all that could lead on to peace! But I did not find it; for I could not achieve it for myself."

---

* See Notes, p. 153.

Chapter III

The Vision

THE deepest sorrow of all came to Sundar Singh, in 1902, at the age of fourteen, when his mother died. Close upon the death of his mother, he lost

SCRIPTURE TESTIMONY
Individuals opposed to the Gospel
ACTS 8:3 · ACTS 9:1-2

also his elder brother, whom he loved very dearly indeed. This double blow made plain to him the utter emptiness of human life apart from God, and the awful desolation of death. For he had never been obliged to look death in the face before in his own home; and now, when this double sorrow swept over him, in an overwhelming flood, it seemed to blot out all happiness. Along with it there came a sense of rebellion against God Himself. Yet while he rebelled, the longing for God, which was deep in his inmost soul, continued.

Whenever he recalled to mind, after he had become a Christian, the tragic sorrow of those early days, a look of pain used to come into his eyes and his voice would break with emotion. For he loved his mother more tenderly than anyone else on earth, and the whole

31

of his life seemed to be shattered when she could be no more with him to encourage and guide him in the right path.

With a young lad, so precocious in his religious temperament, the spiritual shock was more severe even than the mental and physical. He had just reached that impressionable age when such a sorrow would be felt most. The anchorage of his mother's faith, to which his own life had hitherto been so firmly attached, was suddenly severed by a single blow; and he began in his grief to swing to the other extreme of blank despair. He felt that he had now no sure foundation left, and terrible questionings arose in his own mind which could not be laid aside.

At such a crisis of spiritual bewilderment, neither the kindly old Sikh Sadhu nor the Hindu pundit, who taught him Yoga, was able to minister the healing counsel and spiritual help that he so sorely needed. Their own lives had been sheltered from storms, and they were powerless in the presence of this tempestuous upheaval of his soul. It seemed at one time likely to bring shipwreck to all his earlier faith. His father's sorrow was pitiful to witness; but Sundar had no comfort to give him, nor could the father give any consolation to his son.

In certain passages of his own writings, where he describes this time of sorrow, Sundar tells us how the need for some religious assurance of God's presence became more and more imperative. He felt each day that he *must* find out the Truth which lay behind the veil of human existence. At whatever cost, the ultimate questions of life and death had to be faced to the bitter end.

During the two years which followed, there was added to this inward strife one further feature which drove the rebellion in his heart still deeper.

He had gone to a mission primary school, which had just been opened by the American Presbyterian Church in his own village. His wish, in doing so, was to improve his secular education, which had been on the whole neglected. But he found that one of the text-books set for special study was the New Testament. This seemed to him an insidious way of trying to convert him; and, as a high-spirited lad, he was deeply wounded to think that if he continued to attend the school, he would be compelled to read the Christian Scriptures. He determined at last, as a matter of conscience, not to receive religious instruction under compulsion at all. Therefore, at the end of a year, with his father's consent, he left the mission school and entered a Government school instead, even though it was three miles away from his own home.

This encounter with the Christian teachers at the school had roused a latent hostility within him, which was increased by the recent suffering he had gone through owing

SCRIPTURE TESTIMONY
Jesus reveals Himself to an unbeliever
ACTS 9:4-7

to his mother's death. He went to extreme lengths and led a party of youths who used to make attacks on the missionaries themselves whenever they stood up to preach in the bazaar. Sometimes these lads would throw stones and mud at the preachers, and Sundar became their ringleader.

This form of violence in action, which was alien to his nature, came to a head in the middle of December, 1903, when Sundar brought into his father's courtyard a copy of the Christian Gospels and set fire to it in public. Such a public burning of a sacred religious book was an event unheard of before in the village of Rampur.

His father was bewildered and alarmed at his son's extravagant action, which seemed to be altogether unlike him and to have a touch of madness about it.

"Why," he asked his young son, "have you done such a mad thing? Surely you are mad to do a thing like that!"

The boy made no reply, for his mind was truly distraught. He was now over fifteen and was thus rapidly approaching the age of early manhood, for this begins sooner in India than in the West. Youth is a time in which headstrong action is always a dangerous possibility. A wild resolution seemed to possess him that he would either find out the truth that was behind all this agonizing conflict, or else put an end to himself by committing suicide.* Thus the inner struggle went on, unbroken and unappeased.

"Though," he wrote, "according to my own ideas at that time, I thought that I had done a good deed in burning the Gospel, yet my unrest of heart increased, and for the two following days I was very miserable. On the third day, when I could bear it no longer, I got up at three in the morning and prayed that if there was a God at all He would reveal Himself to me."

What followed formed the greatest turning-point in all his life. It must be given in his own words.

"My intention was," he said, "that if I got no satisfaction, I would place my head upon the railway-line when the five o'clock train passed by and kill myself. If I got no satisfaction in this life, I thought I would get it in the next. I was praying and praying but received no answer; and I prayed for half an hour longer hoping to get peace. At 4:30 a.m. I saw something of which I had no idea previously. In the room where I was praying I saw a great light. I thought the place was on fire. I looked round but could find nothing. The thought came to me that this might be an answer that God had sent me. Then as I prayed and looked into the light, I saw the form of the Lord Jesus Christ. It had such an appearance of glory and love! If it had been some Hindu incarnation I would have prostrated myself before it. But it was the Lord Jesus Christ, whom I had been insulting a few days before.

"I felt that a vision like this could not come out of my own imagination. I heard a voice saying in Hindustani: 'How long will you persecute me? I have come to save you; you were praying to know the right way. Why do you not take it?' So I fell at His feet and got this wonderful peace, which I could not get anywhere else. This was the joy I was wishing to get. This was heaven itself.

"When I got up, the vision had all disappeared; but although the vision disappeared, the peace and joy have remained with me ever since.

* For a similar thought in the life of an Indian boy of high imagination, compare *Mahatma Gandhi: His Own Story*, p. 42, published by Macmillan.

"I went off and told my father that I had become a Christian. He told me: 'Go and lie down and sleep. Why, only the day before yesterday you burnt the Bible; and now you say you are a Christian!' I said: 'Well, I have discovered now that Jesus Christ is alive, and have determined to be His follower. To-day I am His disciple, and I am going to serve Him.'"*

Every part of this tremendous experience was so burnt into his young mind that he could never for a moment afterwards question its supreme validity. Others might argue with him about it, when he told the story openly. Some might even make light of it as an hallucination. But for him, it meant such complete assurance of the spiritual reality of what he had seen and heard, that he was ready to prove it by the sacrifice of his own life and all that he held dear.

For it changed his heart so completely that he became a new man in Christ Jesus. Old things had passed away, never to return. The darkness had vanished before the dawn of a glorious new day. Above all, he had found at last that deep, abiding peace for which he had striven so long in vain. For there was now a serenity and steadfast joy in his heart that passed all human understanding. No trial or tribulation on this earth could ever take it away.

"What I saw," he writes, "was no imagination of my own. Up to that moment, I hated Jesus and I did not worship Him. If I had been thinking of Buddha or Krishna, I might have imagined what I saw; for I was in the habit of worshipping them.... No! It was no dream. When you have just had a cold bath, you don't dream! It was a reality—the living Christ. He can turn an enemy into a preacher of the Gospel. He has given me His peace, not for a few hours merely, but for sixteen years— a peace so wonderful that I cannot describe it; but I can testify to its reality."

Sundar Singh absolutely distinguished between this outward event, which came in quite an unexpected manner before his eyes, when he

* Quoted from his Ceylon addresses. The same story was told many times over by the Sadhu in Switzerland and elsewhere. There are slight variations, but the main facts of the incident related are the same.

had no thought of what was going to happen, and his own frequent experience of visions which came, when he was expecting them, through meditation and inner contemplation.

"I have had visions," he writes, "and I know how to distinguish them. But Jesus I have only seen once."

When someone in Switzerland asked him the direct question, whether what he saw on that early morning was objective or subjective, he replied with all possible emphasis that it was no subjective vision, but something objective and external to himself. It came without any conscious imagination on his part.

Indeed, it was so contrary to anything he had ever imagined, that it brought with it a startling shock of blank surprise, leaving him almost stunned by its sudden appearance.

This objective character of the incident was always insisted upon by him, however much others might seek to weaken his evidence, or try to prove to him that it might have come merely from his own excited imagination. He would strongly assert that the difference between an inner vision of the mind and this outward appearance was absolute. He alone could give the final proof in such a matter, and he had offered that proof in its most convincing form by living an entirely different life—so changed, that he had been obliged to face suffering, hardship, persecution, and even death itself, for Christ's sake. He had done so with joy and gladness. Christ's own standard might be applied: "By their fruits ye shall know them. Do men gather grapes from thorns or figs from thistles?"

Was it possible, he asked, for his whole new conduct of life, from that moment forward, to be based on a mere inner picture of the mind? Such things, if self-created, were bound to vanish, but the living experience of Christ had been abiding.

Never at any time did he regard this manifestation of Christ's presence as a matter to boast about, as if he himself had been peculiarly favoured by receiving it. Rather, it humbled him in his inmost heart with a sense of his own wilfulness and rebellion.

This spirit of enmity, which had once possessed him, had only been overcome by Christ when it had reached its furthest point. He had fought against the Christian faith in the most public manner possible, and had burnt the one sacred book that told him the good news concerning the Kingdom of God. Nevertheless, when his inner heart of rebellion was thus most bitter, he had been changed completely and conquered by Christ's own forgiving love.

There were those fortunate ones, he used to say, who had never sinned and rebelled as he had done. There were others who had lived from their childhood with Christ as the One Supreme Reality. These needed no objective proof of what they so truly and inwardly believed. In all humility, Sundar Singh would place himself at the feet of the least of these, as altogether undeserving of the love which God had showered upon him. *They* could receive the blessing of Christ, when He said: "Blessed are they who have not seen and yet have believed."

But he could never win that blessing; for he, like Thomas, had been very slow to believe. His, therefore, was the lesser faith and the lower place in God's Kingdom. With Mary Magdalene, he was among those who had loved much, because they were much forgiven.

Chapter IV

Forsaking All

THE spiritual shock which came to him in the birthpangs of his soul's anguish, could never afterwards be forgotten by Sundar Singh. The victory had been won through the midst of the agony itself. It had been for him, in very truth, a change from death unto life. From the lowest depth of despair, he had risen to a joyful assurance of hope. In the end, as his daily life settled down again to its normal level, he could say with all the fullness of joy: "Thanks be to God who giveth us the victory, through our Lord Jesus Christ."

But in the midst of all this marvellous new-found joy and peace, one fact weighed heavily upon his mind. He had publicly burnt the Christian Scriptures and openly derided the Christian Faith in the presence of his father. This act had been so public that Sardar Sher Singh, who was not a Christian, had rebuked him. Though he knew that Christ's great word of forgiveness had been uttered, pardoning freely this act of rebellion along with all the wrong of the past, yet the shame of it was all the deeper as the knowledge of Christ's forgiveness became more assured.

While I was with him at Kotgarh, some years later, he would still refer to this incident of the burning of the Bible with bitter shame.

Later on, when he was in Europe, he would speak of it as something which could never be forgotten. Many times over he would come back to it in his addresses as the most desperate act of his own rebellion against God. He had thus defied God's love.

"These hands," he would say with remorse, "have burnt in scorn the Word of God. They are the hands of a sinner, whom Christ's love alone has redeemed. My only ground of pardon and forgiveness is the Cross of Jesus, my Lord."

The memory of what had happened deepened in this way his penitence and faith. It was, in reality, the very fullness of his loyalty to Christ which made the thought of his own disloyalty so poignant. "It is always like a thorn in my life," he said on one occasion, "that I was once an enemy of Christ. That thought still humbles me to the dust!"

Thus, by a strange paradox, because he was now so certain that Christ loved him and had forgiven even this sin of denial and derision, for that very reason it had become difficult to forgive himself. The thought of what he had done made him all the more truly penitent. While it revealed to him the depth of his own failure, it also brought home to him, as nothing else could have done, the infinite power of Christ's love.

Just as Christ had sacrificed Himself in love for him, so he, Sundar Singh, must now sacrifice himself in love for Christ. Hereafter his whole life must be in keeping with St. Paul's words: "God forbid that I should glory save in the Cross of our Lord Jesus Christ, by whom the world is crucified unto me and I unto the world."

Those who have themselves gone through the same dark anguish of conversion, can understand best of all both the intensity of his inner conflict and the joy of his release. They can also appreciate how the memory of this special deed of shame still remained behind, impressed upon his own personal life, like a "thorn in the flesh" to buffet him, lest at any time he should be "exalted above measure."

For it had been with him a struggle of life and death, so terrible and vast, that the scars were left upon his memory for many years to come, even after the wounds had been healed; and sometimes when the joy was greatest, the consciousness of his own ungracious deed would return with its sharpest pang of remorse.

There is no more wonderful bond of love in the world than that which binds the soul of man to his Redeemer; and Sundar Singh, immature as he was, and as yet only dimly aware of the amazing inner power of the Christian life, leapt at once to this true conclusion. He was bound to Christ for ever with the cords of love, and therefore he must serve Him as his Lord.

Many days were passed in solitude and inner communion, during which the full sense of Christ's forgiveness came home to him more and more in the silence of his own soul. He received, along with this sense of forgiveness, the commission from his Divine Saviour to go out and tell others what great things had been done, whereby his whole life had been redeemed for service. Seeds were then sown in his heart which were to bear fruit afterwards in his repeated journeys to Tibet.

We have to bear in mind, at this point, the fact that Sundar Singh was not yet a grown-up man. He was still hardly more than fifteen years of age; and though early manhood comes quickly in the East, the authority of the home is very strong indeed, and the father's word is law. Sardar Sher Singh was head of the joint family, and this made the weight of his authority all the more powerful. Sundar knew well that for a lad of his age to challenge the whole family, by declaring himself a Christian, would mean an intolerable offence. It would seem to strike at the root of all parental discipline and of that loyalty to ancestral religion of which the Sikhs are rightly so proud. It was certain to be misunderstood and was also likely neither to be forgotten nor forgiven. Yet this is what he at once determined to do. Furthermore, we need to keep in mind that he was entirely alone during these days. He had no one to consult who could advise or sympathize with him. All that he was about to do was done with one Companion only at his side—Christ Himself.

To declare to the world what had taken place, and to explain the change in his own inner life, was to meet with incredulity on every side and to be treated as one who was insane. In his own home, since his mother's death, there was no one who could understand him. His brother, who was still living, had no sympathy whatever with his spiritual struggles. His sister also, absorbed in her own religious devotions, seems to have been unable to understand him. His uncle and his father both regarded him as mad, and they possessed what was to them convincing proof of the fact. Had he not only a few days before actually burnt the Christian Scriptures? What could be more insane than to do such a public act one day and then declare himself a Christian only three days later? The boy, they would say, had always been eccentric. Now his eccentricity had taken the more violent turn of madness. His mind had become utterly unhinged.

Such were the thoughts and sentiments which came naturally to his father and uncle, when Sundar Singh declared himself before them both to be a follower of Christ.

"Leave him alone," was the advice of his shrewd old father. "If he is left alone he will soon get over his madness."

So they left him alone at first. But it was all in vain. Sundar stood his ground, even when the whole family refused to eat with him unless he gave up his absurd idea of becoming a Christian. Those who had joined with him in deriding the Christians before began to persecute him in turn, but he paid them no heed.

SCRIPTURE TESTIMONY

God brings comfort and peace to the persecuted

ACTS 23:11

Everything was done at first by persuasion and entreaty, and then at last by the most cogent appeals to his pride as a member of the Sikh community. The leading members of his family, finding other appeals vain, pressed him at least to give way so far as to refrain from openly declaring himself a Christian. The inducement was offered to him that he might remain a secret believer, without any open profession of his Christian faith.

This last trial of all was, perhaps, the hardest that he was called upon to bear; for there were many things that made the temptation of secrecy especially urgent and plausible in his case. He was not yet of legal age to act alone, and therefore he might easily excuse himself from making an open confession until he grew older. But an inner voice seemed always to tell him that he must not deny his Lord, and he remained firm.

When at last his father and uncle knew that nothing would induce him to be silent, they adopted sterner measures. They threatened him with public exclusion from the family and at last carried out their own threat. He was also excommunicated by his own act from the Sikh religion.

"I remember," he writes, "the night when I was driven out of my home—the first night. When I came to know my Saviour, I told my father and my brother and my other relations. At first they did not take much notice; but afterwards they thought that it was a great dishonour that I should become a Christian, and so I was driven out of my home. The first night I had to spend, in cold weather, under a tree. I had had no such experience. I was not used to living in such a place without a shelter. I began to think: 'Yesterday and before that I used to live in the midst of luxury at my home; but now I am shivering here, and hungry and thirsty and without a shelter, with no warm clothes and no food? I had to spend the whole night under the tree. But I remember the wonderful joy and peace in my heart, the presence of my Saviour. I held my New Testament in my hand. I remember that night as my first night in heaven. I remember the wonderful joy that made me compare that time with the time when I was living in a luxurious home. In the midst of luxuries and comfort I could not find peace in my heart. The presence of the Saviour changed the suffering into peace. Ever since then I have felt the presence of the Saviour."*

It was legally necessary for him to remain till he was sixteen years of age before he could be baptized. During the interval he went to Ludhiana and stayed with Dr. Wherry and Dr. Fife. But since there

---

* *The Bible in the World,* June, 1920, quoted by Streeter and Appasamy, p. 10.

was some danger of an outbreak of mob violence if he was baptized so near his own home as Ludhiana, he was taken to Simla and there baptized on his birthday, September 3rd, 1905, when he had reached the legal age of sixteen years.

The Rev. J. Redman, of Simla, had spent his whole ministry in India, carrying on with wonderful humility and devotion his Master's work of love. No more gentle and tender father in God could have been given to Sundar than this aged servant of Christ. His home was always open, and a "prophet's chamber" was kept for Sundar himself to occupy whenever he passed through Simla. What he owed to Mr. Redman and his wife can hardly be told in words. On both sides it was a profound joy to meet thus from time to time in fellowship, communion and prayer. Mr. Redman is now dead and Canon Chandu Lal, one of the Sadhu's closest friends, has taken his place.

When Sundar came to Simla, in 1905, as a Christian convert, altogether unknown, except by the missionaries at Ludhiana, Mr. Redman questioned him thoroughly concerning his faith in Christ, and afterwards wrote about him briefly as follows: "I was deeply impressed by his sincerity. I examined him carefully, and asked him a great many questions about the chief facts of the Gospel. Sundar Singh replied to my entire satisfaction, and he evinced even then an extraordinary knowledge of the life and teaching of Christ. Then I inquired into his personal experience of Christ as his Saviour.. Again I was more than satisfied. And I told him I would be very glad to baptize him on the following day, which was a Sunday. He replied that he desired to be baptized because it was the will of Christ; but he felt so sure that the Lord had called him to witness, that even if I could not see my way to baptize him, he would have to go out and preach."

It has been pointed out by Dr. Heiler that the twenty-third Psalm was used as a part of the service in St. Thomas's Church, Simla, when Sundar Singh was openly admitted to membership in the Body of Christ. The opening words were prophetic of the life which he now chose to live:

"The Lord is my Shepherd,
Therefore can I lack nothing."

Perhaps these words would have been the one text which he would have chosen for that solemn moment of dedication and blessing. He often referred to them in later years; for this Psalm of the Good Shepherd and the fifty-third chapter of Isaiah were his two favourite passages in the Old Testament, which moulded and fashioned his whole life.

Chapter V

Discipleship

O NE of the greatest difficulties which had to be faced when
Sundar left his father's house and became a member of the
Christian Church, was the strangely "foreign" aspect of the
daily life which was led by Indian Christians.

Their modes of worship, the church buildings, their very dress
and food and manner of conduct, all spoke to him of an alien faith.
There was no intimate touch with his own motherland. He had been
told often enough, before his conversion, that Indian Christians
were "foreigners" (Feringi), and that they were introducing "foreign"
ways; and now the experiences which he met every day, in mission
compounds and boarding-schools, seemed to justify that complaint.
When, at a much later date, he was questioned about these things,
he used one of his picture-phrases, which vividly illustrated how he
felt the change. "The Water of Life," he said sadly, "has hitherto been
offered to thirsting souls in India in a European vessel. Only when
it is given in an Eastern bowl will it be accepted by simple men and
women who seek the truth."

Therefore it was with a bewilderment almost akin to repugnance
that he now for the first time came into immediate contact with

47

those very Christians whom he had, for a long time past, despised as alien to his own people. He found it exceedingly difficult at first to overcome this feeling of antagonism, and his proud nature as a Sikh rebelled against the humiliations from which he had to suffer. Only the intense reality of his living communion with Christ, as his Lord and Master, enabled him to hold fast throughout. The extraordinary gentleness and humility which everyone noticed in his character during the later years of his life, came in a great measure from this severe inward discipline and self-restraint which he put upon himself in order to overcome his pride.

That understanding sympathy, however, for which he craved so much during these first years as a Christian, was offered to him in full measure by some of the oldest missionaries, who realized his loneliness of heart. The Rev. J. Redman, one of the humblest men I have ever known, was his true supporter. Mr. Redman's wife was equally helpful. The two older missionaries at Ludhiana, Dr. Wherry and Dr. Fife, were also among those who encouraged him in this time of need. Still further, the loving companionship of S. E. Stokes gave him much valued assistance, for they lived like brothers together.

A touching story was told me which revealed in a single act, instinct with Indian sentiment, how deeply the love of those European missionaries, who had helped him in most of his own country, had filled his mind with grateful thoughts. When Willie Hindle was his companion in England, he brought him one day to his own father's house. Sundar immediately stooped down and touched the old man's feet. He then thanked him with deep emotion for having surrendered his son to India for Christ's sake.

From the very first, Sundar Singh had a remarkable faculty for making friends, close to his own heart, among those whose love for Christ was altogether akin to his own. This stood him in good stead during these first critical years for he was helped and carried forward over these initial difficulties, in some measure, by the few friends he had made.

Nevertheless, in spite of all that was done to relieve him, the sympathy of individuals could hardly dispel the sense of strangeness which he felt so acutely in his new surroundings. Indeed, when he entered as a student the Christian High School at Ludhiana and lived there as a boarder, this very kindness of the missionaries became, in some ways, a source of embarrassment to him; for it was resented by the older Christian boys, who found Sundar held in greater regard by their teachers than they were themselves.

The present headmaster of the school at Ludhiana, who was then Sundar's fellow student in the same school, has written to me a singularly interesting letter, describing the general effect of his presence upon the other boys.

"Sundar Singh," he relates, "joined the Christian Boys' Boarding-School, Ludhiana, late in the year 1904. Dr. Wherry was Principal, but shortly afterwards his duties were taken over by Dr. Fife. Sundar boarded at the Matron's table, and we all looked up to him as a special boy.

"He remained a special and unique boy all through the days of his school life, and, of course, he was destined to be a unique personality in the world in later years. Because of his reflective nature and the religious trend of his mind he attracted only a few friends. In fact, the special attention he received from our superiors made him an object of envy to us. He could hardly be coaxed to participate in games, or in any other of the school activities. But the boys used to make him one of themselves by playing an occasional joke on him.

"Our Matron was an English lady, who spoke very little Urdu. Sundar Singh did not know English. We told him that if the Matron offered him something he did not want, he should answer politely: 'No, thank you.'

"One day at the table the Matron asked him whether he had been baptized, and he answered very politely: 'No, thank you.'

"Whenever in later life I had the joy of meeting him, we used to recall this incident with hearty laughter. Sundar Singh once remarked that he had laughed more during a certain hour that he had spent with me than he had done for several years.

"On one occasion, I had the privilege of coming into closer touch with him. Because there had been an outbreak of cholera, my brother and I were sent to spend the summer holidays at Ambala City with the Rev. Ghulam Masih. Sundar Singh was also sent there, and I learnt something of the depth of his religious nature. I began also to respect his religious sentiments, though I still envied him somewhat because the Padre Sahib always seemed to take more interest in him than he did in us.

"Now, however, as I look back, I think of Sundar Singh in terms of the Boy Christ, who, instead of participating in the 'Id* festivities, was found sitting with the learned Jewish Doctors, both hearing them and asking them questions. It was not they who took an interest in Him, but He who commanded their attention.

"As we were returning to school after the vacation, we had an example of the rebellion of Sundar Singh's free soul against rules and regulations. Without any permission he slipped off the train at Doraha and went to see his relatives. After a few days he returned to school, but this was not for long. For on October 3rd, 1905, a month after his baptism, he took his discharge certificate and disappeared, only to reappear on the world's stage as a Sadhu."

SCRIPTURE TESTIMONY
Do not retaliate, instead behave honorably
ROMANS 12:17
Forgiving your persecutor
MATTHEW 5:44

The "rebellion" which is noted by this kindly headmaster was repeated at a later stage in his life, which may be anticipated here. In the year 1909, the Bishop of Lahore, Dr. Lefroy, to whom he was very deeply attached, offered to ordain him to the sacred ministry if he would prepare for Holy Orders at the Theological College in Lahore. Out of deference to the Bishop, whom he loved, he accepted the offer of

---

*   The word a "'Id" is used by Muslims for their chief religious festivals

theological training that was made to him and studied under Canons Wood and Wigram in the Divinity School.

But here again he soon found himself out of his element and a stranger among the students, who were being prepared for the ministry. As a Sadhu, his standard of living was quite different from theirs, and his devotional life was also of a different type from the regulated services which were held in the Divinity School. He did not find it at all easy to get on with the students, and for the most part lived in his own small room apart, meeting them only at meal times and at the stated hours of prayer.

On their side there seems to have been something of the same resentment which he met at Ludhiana. For the ordinary Divinity students seemed to feel all the while that the Sadhu was setting up a new standard superior to their own, and that they were being silently condemned by his presence among them.

Sundar did his utmost to avoid anything that might be regarded as censorious and remained humbly waiting to win their goodwill and affection; but this did not appear for some time.

One day, a student, who had been a ringleader in this resentful treatment, saw Sundar apart under a tree, sitting alone, and went up quite close to him without being noticed by him. To his great surprise, he found that Sundar was in tears, pouring out his heart to God in earnest supplication on behalf of this very student who had thus come near. He was praying that anything which he himself might have done amiss might be forgiven, and that true love might be established between them.

The student, when he heard this prayer, was so overcome, that he discovered himself to Sundar on the spot and asked his forgiveness, and they became close friends. This devoted companion of Sundar's at the Divinity School is still living and working in the Punjab. His ministry in the Church has owed its depth and power to his conversion at Lahore. He has written out for me a full account of the whole incident, and it is from his own words that I have told the story.

Whenever it was possible to do so, I used to visit Sundar Singh in his room at Lahore during his time at the Divinity School. For I felt, from the first time that I met him there, that he was very unhappy. Fortunately, my University duties called me often to Lahore at that period, and I would make a point of going round to see him in order to give him good cheer. He seemed to me like some bird of the forest, beating its wings in vain against the bars of a cage. For the joyous, open freedom at Kotgarh, with the clear sky overhead and the solitude of the hills round about, had been left behind. It was almost as if his wings had been clipped, and I felt deeply distressed about him when I saw what was happening, as though a tragedy was being acted out before my eyes.

Fortunately, the Bishop himself, as well as the Sadhu, soon discovered the strange mistake that was being made; and it was corrected before it became too late. For a question arose whether, if he were ordained, he would be able to preach freely before any Christian congregation and also receive the sacrament with them. The Bishop felt definitely that if he were ordained for work in his own diocese, this would strictly limit his ministry to the Anglican Communion.

Such a narrow, unlooked-for decision, from the Bishop, whom he loved, came as a great shock to Sundar. He had never even thought of such restrictions before. Now that he was faced with this alternative, he at once realized that to be constrained in such a manner would not be in keeping with his vocation as a Christian Sadhu. It also appeared to him not to be in accordance with the universal character of Christ's teaching.

So in the end, after much prayer and earnest communion with God, he decided to remain unfettered by any ecclesiastical bonds, and he observed this principle of spiritual freedom to the very end.

An interesting story is related, in this connexion, about a conversation he had with the Archbishop of Canterbury while he was in England. Sundar told the Archbishop quite frankly that he had made it a rule of his life to preach whenever he was asked to do so, whatever

the congregation might be: for he had crossed the bounds of all denom-
inations, joining in full communion with all those who loved the Lord
Jesus Christ in sincerity. The Archbishop said to him in reply: "*That is
all right for you,*" and the general mind of Christians would be inclined
to agree with the Archbishop.*

Just as the Prophets of old kept their freedom intact, and by that
very liberty of action were able to go out at a moment's notice in
order to obey God's call, however hard it might be, so the Sadhu
retained that "liberty of prophesying" which is one of the true marks
of a living Church.

Perhaps a personal reference may be allowed at this place in the
memoir which I am now writing; for these special years, when great
decisions were being made in the Punjab, were full of painful unset-
tlement in my own life. Nothing less had to be decided, once and for
all, than the whole future of my work in relation to the Indian Christian Church.** Sundar Singh's living witness, which was continually
before my eyes, did very much to shape the course that I was led at
last to pursue. Though I did not take counsel from him as I did from
Principal Rudra at Delhi, his personal example was continually present
before my mind, and I found it impossible to retain my old position
in the College at Delhi, where I had been working on conventional
lines. Furthermore, I found it impossible to separate myself by any
denominational barriers from fellow Christians who were ready to
join with me in devotion to our common Lord.

In this chapter I have been obliged to carry the story forward in order
to illustrate the Sadhu's intense emphasis on retaining his spiritual
freedom. It is a memoir that I am writing rather than a consecutive
history of the Sadhu's life, and therefore I shall go backwards and
forwards in the narrative again and again.

---

*   This incident is told in *The Message of Sadhu Sundar Singh,* p. 18.
**   See *What I Owe to Christ,* Chapter X.

Chapter VI

The Homeless Wanderer

S UNDAR Singh had already begun to wear the Sadhu's dress when
I first saw him at Kotgarh. He took this step almost immediately
after his baptism and thus fulfilled, as a Christian, the desire that
had always been nearest to his mother's heart.

His homeless condition as
a wanderer, "carrying neither
purse nor scrip," had been literally thrust upon him; but he had
welcomed it with gladness for
Christ's sake, as a way of learning to be His true disciple. For

SCRIPTURE TESTIMONY
Kingdom messengers sent *out with no provision*
MATTHEW 10:5-15 · LUKE 9:1-6 · LUKE 10:1-20

Sundar's father together with all his friends and relations, had banished
him from home when once he had taken the final step which made him
outwardly as well as inwardly a Christian.

The choice at that time lay before him, either to depend on some mission
for his support until he could obtain an income of his own, or else to begin
life afresh as a wandering Sadhu, living without any home or shelter from
day to day, as the birds of the air and the flowers of the field, casting all
his care upon God, who cared for him and loved him as His own child.

55

As soon as the choice was thus presented to his mind, there was not a moment's hesitation. For his mother's ardent desire, his own deep longing, and his new idea of what true discipleship of Christ involved, all appeared to him to combine together in pointing to the life of a Sadhu as the one which he was now called upon to follow. Therefore, he had practically taken his choice even before he joined the Christian Church.

While this decision came to him instinctively as the right thing to do, the fact remains that it was an almost revolutionary step for any young Indian Christian to take at that time. For current ideas were tending to shape themselves more and more in the opposite direction. A desire to make rapid material progress had weakened the Christian conception of renunciation within the Church in the Punjab. It was urged that the Christian faith represented the fullness of human life; that material things were to be consecrated to Christ's service, and not to be abandoned altogether. The Hindu idea of renunciation, it was asserted, differed fundamentally from the Christian.

While there was a certain element of truth in this, it also tended to lead on to self-deception by leaving out of sight renunciation altogether.

Sundar Singh himself knew very little concerning all these cross-currents of thought, which hardly reached him in the Himalayas. He kept steadily on his way and soon had the great good fortune to meet S. E. Stokes, who had set out quite independently from a different angle on a somewhat similar quest. Not only did Stokes give him the loving companionship which he needed at this time, but still further he set forward a conception of the Sadhu life which brought it more into living touch with the Franciscan ideal. For Stokes was endeavouring to follow Christ along the pathway of poverty and renunciation followed by St. Francis of Assisi.

Sundar had probably heard very little about St. Francis before he met Samuel Stokes. As a Sadhu he was keeping as near as possible to the ancient Indian tradition by abandoning all earthly ties in his search for God. He added the one supreme motive which transformed everything. For it was the constraining power of the love of Christ which supported him and gave him inward peace. He was a Bhakta of the Lord Jesus.

When, however, he came into closest touch with Samuel Stokes, immediately he saw that the service of God is not complete if it stands entirely alone. The service of man must be absorbed within the divine service as an integral factor. In the ancient Indian ideal, the human spirit goes forth in utter detachment from human society in order to find God. With St. Francis, on the other hand, God Himself is found through the service of the poor. A common devotion to God's poor is itself a joyous pathway leading to the beatific vision. In this, the Franciscan ideal was true to the mind of Christ.

Sundar, with Stokes as his helper, made a very brave attempt to combine these two ideals. He loved solitude with all his soul; but he sought to unite it with the love of those who suffered pain. He beheld Christ in vision and imagination among those that were most afflicted; he heard His voice saying: "I was afflicted in their afflictions." Thus his ardent devotion to Christ made him come away, even out of his deepest meditations, to serve them.

Yet he never became involved in any outward organization of human service; and I have already pointed out how instinctively he shrank back when any attempt was made to get him to become an ordained minister of any Christian Church. It is equally interesting to note how this deepest Indian instinct for solitude—"alone with the Alone"—reasserted itself as he grew older. His whole inner nature shrank back from a life absorbed in busy activity, which left no time for prayer. The inner life remained essential with him up to the very end.

He took, as we have seen, no vow of obedience to any earthly superior: he submitted to no rule of life framed by the Head of an Order: he joined no outward society, except that of the Christian Church itself, nor did he advise others to do so. Though he greatly desired to throw in his lot with the Brotherhood of the Imitation, out of his great love for Brother Stokes and Brother Western, he remained even there unattached. While his whole heart went out in sympathy towards those who became members of the Order, he felt more and more that his own true vocation did not lie in that direction.

In his addresses delivered in Switzerland, Sundar used a remarkable illustration from the mountain scenery which he loved best of all in the Himalayas. It appeared to him to carry its own lesson with it.

"The streams," he said, "in the Himalayan Mountains, as they rush forth from the pure white snows, cut their own course. Each one has its own appointed path which it follows down the mountainside. That rushing torrent of pure water from the heights is the true symbol of the Christian life as it comes direct from Christ Himself.

"But when the same waters reach the plains, they carry the mud along with them, and their tributaries are diverted into channels by artificial means, forming irrigation canals. These, too, have their uses, but they depend on the streams which flow from the mountain heights for their perennial supply of fresh and living water."

Even so, he would add, there may be the need of organizations formed by men to make the Christian life spread itself far and wide among the masses of mankind but the pure rushing streams from the mountain heights must never be allowed to run dry.

Thus, while in no way minimizing the value of a fully regulated Christian life, Sundar Singh felt that his own devotion to his Master led him to a more individual and solitary course. The life in Christ which he had been called upon to follow, must be on the heights, like a rushing mountain stream.

Certainly, in those early days, when the ardour of his devotion was at its height, this spontaneous and creative freedom of the spirit was characteristic of the Sadhu as we knew him. He would be here one day and away the next. Very early in the morning, before daybreak, he would start on some new journey, leaving a single word behind that he had felt the call and had gone. Then he would reappear as suddenly, no one knew from whence.

While telling the story of those early days, and recounting his own spiritual companionship with Sundar Singh, S. E. Stokes wrote as follows:

> "Some weeks after I had changed my life, an Indian Christian was moved to join me. He was a convert from the Sikhs and had been travelling about the country as a Christian Sadhu for more than a year before he took the vows and put on the robe of a Friar. At a later date I hope to write an account of him and the work he has done, so will not at present enter upon the subject. When my work took me to the plains, he remained in charge of our interests up in the mountains, and laboured so faithfully and with such effect that all were astonished. His work has been far better than my own, and although he is scarcely more than a boy, he has suffered hunger, cold, sickness, and even imprisonment for his Master.
>
> "Before leaving him, I will tell of one thing which illustrates his saintly spirit and his fitness for the Friar's life. We had been some

SCRIPTURE TESTIMONY
Counted worthy of suffering disgrace for the Name
ACTS 5:41

> hundreds of miles back into the interior, and had been forced to pass through some very unhealthy country. Sundar Singh was attacked by fever day after day, and also by acute indigestion. At length one night, as we were trudging along, he became so bad that he could no longer walk and fell almost fainting on the road.
>
> "Our way ran through the mountains, and there was a bank by the side of it. To this I dragged him and set him against it in such a way that his head might be higher than his feet. He was trembling with the chill which precedes the fever, and his face was drawn with the pain caused by his stomach trouble.

I was anxious because we were alone and on foot and the weather was very cold.

"Bending close to his ear, I asked him how he was feeling. I knew that he would never complain, but I was unprepared for the answer which I received. He opened his eyes and smiled absently, then in a voice almost too low to be heard said: 'I am very happy: how sweet it is to suffer for His sake!' This spirit is the key-note of his life and the dominating influence in all he does."*

In the hot weather of 1906, I had been taking duty in the Simla Hills, at Sanawar, owing to an illness which made it impossible for me to remain in the plains during that season of the year. Sanawar is not far from the leper home at Sabathu, where Stokes and Sundar Singh were staying. For some reason, however, I was not able to come into close touch with them at that time, though I heard constantly about them. But in the following year, it was with the utmost eagerness that Principal Rudra and I seized the opportunity of going out together to Kotgarh and thus meeting them at last face to face. I have already told the story of that meeting.**

During the years that followed, right on up to 1911, Rudra and his sons used to go regularly with me to Bareri, above Kotgarh. Our first inquiry each time, when we arrived from Simla, was about Sundar Singh and S. E. Stokes, and also concerning the company of crippled boys whom they used to bring with them each year to the Hills. For they collected, in the manner of the Gospel, the maimed, the lame, the halt and the blind, along with certain children of leper parents, in order to form a summer camp for them in the Hills.

A happier company of children it would be impossible to meet, and they won our heart's affection whenever we were able to be with them. At Bareri, which was only two miles distant, we were near enough to make it easy to run backwards and forwards, up and down the hill-side,

---

*   *The East and the West,* April, 1908.
**   See p. 2.

in order to join their company. While at other times it might not be possible to see Sundar Singh for more than a few days, because of his wandering life, here at Kotgarh we could get more frequent opportunities of meeting; and it was easier also to speak about the subjects which we both had so deeply at heart.

Not often, however, could he remain with us for long, even at Kotgarh. For he would wander about the Hills and then return. On our arrival, early in July, we were likely to hear the news that he had already started out along the Road, and was on his way to Tibet, and that nothing had been heard of him since.

During these vacations at Bareri, on rare occasions while Rudra and I would be spending, our mornings in preparing our College lectures, it would be a very great delight to us when Sundar Singh came in unexpectedly from one of these long Hill journeys, and called to see us on his way down to Kotgarh. At other times, late in the afternoon, when our work was over, we used to go down the hill-side to see him in the house where he stayed.

The growing friendship with Sundar Singh, which was thus slowly maturing year after year, led on naturally to return visits paid by him to our home in the College where Rudra and I lived together. It would mean a time of great joy to both of us when he arrived. Susil Rudra's two sons, Shudhir and Ajit, were great favourites with him; for he was always devoted to children, and these two boys were specially loved by him. They would run up to him and take his hands in theirs and ask about the cripple children by name, and how they were getting on at school; what villages he had been able to visit, and how he had been received. It was at such times as these that Sundar was at his very best. For the childheart came out in him without any restraint. All his natural reticence and reserve broke down, and he was at home with them at once in joyous freedom and merry laughter. He would go on talking all day with them, if only he had the time.

Susil Rudra enjoyed these visits most of all. He was a perfect host, and his heart always went out to Sundar Singh with a kindly, fatherly love. Their devotion to Christ united them as no earthly bond could do and drew their hearts together. No one, I believe, among Indian Christians, was dearer to Susil than this young heroic follower of Christ; and no son could have loved his father more than Sundar Singh loved him. While many things in the Indian Christian Church used to sadden Susil, as unworthy of the name of Christ crucified, the compensation came when he could welcome such a true follower of his Master as Sundar Singh. He felt that if only the witness to Christ in India could take this form of devoted sacrifice, then all would be well.

At that time we had a remarkable group of young Indian Christians at Delhi, studying under Principal Rudra. They have since gained distinction in many walks of life. The deepest Christian influence upon them, when they were at College, was the contact they were able to maintain with Sadhu Sundar Singh.

> **SCRIPTURE TESTIMONY**
>
> *Demonstration of who is our neighbor*
>
> LUKE 10:29-37

One of the senior students of our party returned to us late one evening, carrying on his back a Hillman, who was in the last stage of a terribly infectious disease. He had found him in an unfrequented place at the edge of the jungle, where he had been lying neglected, possibly for some days. So without a thought of danger, he had carried him on his back, single-handed, for nearly two miles along a difficult mountain track. Even the physical feat was remarkable; but the moral stamina that made him ready to risk a dangerous disease, while others had "passed by on the other side," was more noteworthy still. Only because, at that time, he was living with the Sadhu, did the inspiration come to him with such compelling force as to make him act in this manner. Still further, the humility and reticence with which this brave deed was done, were themselves a reflection of Sundar's Christian spirit.

Chapter VII

The Road to Tibet

A T Delhi, during these eventful years, new problems were springing up every day, within the Christian Church of the Punjab,
which clamoured for solution. Further delay was impossible if
the young community of Christians was to remain vigorous and strong.

One of the greatest of these difficulties confronted us in St. Stephen's
College itself. The Christian youths who came to us from every part
of the Punjab for university education, were certain to be leaders of
the Church in the future; for whether they entered the ministry or
remained as laymen, they were bound to occupy prominent positions.
The community was still in its infancy, and very few members of it
had reached the university standard.

But a tradition had grown up which had already become fraught
with very serious consequences. Sons of Indian Christians, whatever
their qualifications, could easily obtain monetary assistance if only they
could pass the Matriculation. This was due, in the main, to kindly help
which came from abroad. The ease, however, with which such help was
obtained, defeated its own object. It created a sense of dependence on
outside support which became demoralizing. It led on to the further
expectation that everything would be done by us in College to advance

the worldly prospects of our students. The nerve-centre of self-sacrifice was severed wherever thoughts like these prevailed.

Christ's message of the Cross was difficult to explain in such an atmosphere; for the Cross had become to many of our students just what it appeared to the Greeks—mere foolishness.* Yet we, who were their teachers, had been responsibly commissioned to show that Christ crucified was in truth "the power of God and the wisdom of God."

This difficulty became acute because our own conventional lives, as members of the College staff, did not impress our students by their self-denial. We did our work surrounded by too much outward comfort. Thus we were working in a vicious circle, from which it seemed impossible to escape; for it did not appear possible either to Principal Rudra or to those of us who were on his staff immediately to change our style of living, though we often talked the matter over.

Just at this point, the Sadhu came quite simply and almost unconsciously to our rescue. While he was in Delhi with Mr. Rudra, he used to spend the greater part of his spare time with the Christian students in the Hostel. They sat up with him into the long hours of the night, and very soon became intensely eager to go up to Kotgarh and live with him there, so that they might catch something of his own brave spirit. He did what no older man could have done; for he was young like themselves.

The change which came in this manner was marvellous to witness. One of the students, a cricketer and athlete, gave up assured prospects in Government service for directly Christian work. Another made up his mind to enter the ministry of the Church for a life of sacrifice and devotion. When one of the College sweepers, who was an "untouchable," was ill, one of those who had come most of all under the influence of the Sadhu, went into the "sweepers' quarters" and stayed with him and nursed him through his illness. Such a thing had never happened in the history of the College before.

What, it may be asked, was the attraction that made such a wonderful change? Nothing that was merely second-rate could

---

*   1 Corinthians 1:23

possibly have effected it. No mode of living, half in comfort, half in self-denial, could have worked such a miracle. But Sundar Singh's life *could* stand the test. It was reckless in its self-spending. He had counted the cost. The Cross was not preached only, but lived—and that made all the difference.

In Sundar Singh's own handwriting I have a manuscript and a small calendar giving an account of one of his many journeys to the Tibetan border on its Western side. In the calendar he has jotted down against each day throughout July and August the place where he passed the night. The facts recorded in this manuscript are not so marvellous as those that occurred on other occasions, and yet the hardships he encountered made it a continual wonder that he ever came through alive. It was the story of journeys like these, simply told by the Sadhu himself, which kindled the hearts of the students at Delhi as they sat listening to him half-way through the night.

This special journey took place in 1919, and was therefore later than those College days which I have been recalling. But the record is typical of all the earlier journeys also, and may well be taken as an example.

"At the beginning of July," he writes, "I set out for Tibet by the Hindustan-Tibet Road, taking a Tibetan Christian with me whose name was Thaniyat. We started from Kotgarh, which is nearly a hundred and thirty miles from the border."

He then mentions different villages at which he stopped "to proclaim the Gospel of Jesus to the people," until at last he came to the border of Tibet. There were only shepherds to be seen for many miles around, across the border, and no human habitation. Therefore both of them were obliged to sleep in the open. Farther on, the cold became intense, especially at nights; for they were climbing over a very difficult pass. Many people had actually died in the snow, which lay on the ground throughout the year. The pass itself rose to nearly 19,000 feet, and they saw three dead bodies on the road. When they crossed the pass at that high altitude, they found their breathing becoming difficult, and the beating of their hearts sounded with a heavy thud in their ears. Glaciers had to be crossed, with crevasses, but by God's good grace they both came through in safety.

When they had reached a village called Mudh, on the other side, they were received with great kindness. The headman of the village brought the chief Lama to come and take food with the Sadhu. He knew a little Hindustani and "heard the word of God with gladness." Other people also were ready to listen to the Gospel. Thus they went on from one village to another until they reached a Tibetan monastic centre, called Kee Gunpa, where there was a temple with four hundred Lamas. They remained with the head Lama for two days. "Although," writes the Sadhu, "he did not put us to any suffering, yet he carried on a great controversy with us."

Singh then goes on to explain the various kinds of dangers and difficulties encountered on their forward journey. The currents of the rivers, which had to be crossed on foot, were often very fast, and great boulders were continually washed down, which made even swimming difficult. In the icy water the body of the swimmer became quite numbed. Thaniyat was very nearly drowned.

There was also continual trouble about food. Only tea was provided, which was drunk with salt and butter, and along with this they were given parched barley. "Sometimes," writes the Sadhu quaintly, "the barley is prepared in such a way that even a horse or a mule will not touch it!" Then he adds the following significant words:

"There is only one comfort in the midst of all these troubles. They are all endured for the sake of the Cross. For my sake, Christ left heaven and endured the suffering of the Cross. If I for His sake, in order to save souls, have left India and have come to Tibet, that is no great matter. But if I did not go, that would be sad indeed: for it was surely my duty to go."

He found the houses of the Tibetans very small and dirty. The people themselves were dirty also, and their clothes made of wool became quite black with dirt, because they were never washed. When the Sadhu went to clean his own clothes in a stream, the people looked on with wonder. The chief Lama rebuked him for it, saying: "There is no harm in evil people washing their clothes, but for holy men to wash—that is a very bad thing indeed!"

Though they had many hardships to encounter on this journey, they did not have such trials to bear as had been met with on other occasions. The Lamas, instead of persecuting them, received them in a friendly manner. They gave them, as usual, salted tea with butter and parched barley for their food, and helped the Sadhu in other ways. He relates with a touch of humour how one day a kindly Lama, seeing that he had some trouble because his hair was too long, took a big instrument, with which wool was cut off the sheep's backs, and used it on his head.

"We went on from Kiwar," he relates, "and had good opportunities of preaching in other villages. But the people were very few in number; thieves and robbers also abound, keeping the countryside in a state of panic. One good man said to me: 'You ought not to go about without a sword or a gun. For this is a dreadful place to live in, and many people have been murdered.'

SCRIPTURE TESTIMONY
God is faithful to keep us from evil
2 THESSALONIANS 3:1-3

"'I have only my Bible and my blanket,' I replied. 'The Word of God is my sword. The Lord of Life is with me, and He will deliver me.'

"Through the mercies of God, I came out of it all quite safely. In that panic-stricken region, I preached the Word of God. Indeed, those very robbers who had committed murders came in and stayed with us and did not do us the least bit of harm. Yet there were actually people present there who had lost a leg or a hand through the cruelty of these bandits, who had mutilated them in this manner. Others had even been murdered. But the Lord brought us through in safety."

The Sadhu notices that in spite of their addiction to violence, and their dirty way of living, the Tibetans are at heart a very kindly and religious folk. The custom of each family was to make the eldest son carry on the work of the house while the rest of the sons became Lamas. He mentions also the famous Tibetan hermits, some of whom he actually visited.

"They shut themselves up," he says, "in a dark cell. Some remain in this condition for a number of years. Some stay in darkness for their whole lives. They never see the sun and never come out. They sit inside and turn a prayer-wheel. Thus they live, just as if they were in the grave. On one side of their dark cells they make a small hole through which people put food for them to eat. I tried hard to talk with them, but did not get permission. I could only throw, through the hole, some passages of Scripture for them to read.

"From these hermits I learnt a great lesson. For these people go through all this suffering to gain that which is nothing at all. They do it to reach Nirvana, which holds out no prospect of a future life and heavenly joy, but only leads to the extermination of life and spirit and all desires. This is their idea of salvation. How much more ought we to serve Christ and lay hold on eternal life, and in His service joyfully take up the Cross for His sake, who has given and will give us His heavenly blessing!"

The Sadhu ends this short narrative of his tour by explaining that because it was already late in the year when he started, he was obliged to return towards the end of August. He had found the tiny band of Christians on the Tibetan border whom he visited doing well. This was a matter of deep thankfulness to him, as they were very isolated and had no instructor. He hoped to be able to take one of them back to India and give him a good training so that he might return to teach his own people.

After returning from adventures such as these, and meeting once more the students from our College, Sundar Singh would so inspire them with his own courageous spirit that for many weeks afterwards they would speak to one another about him, and plan expeditions to the Hills so as to be with him on one of his journeys into the interior. On some occasions one or two of them would start with him, but

the difficulties of the way would become too great and they would
be obliged to return. Nevertheless, at Kotgarh itself, whenever he was
known to be there, they would eagerly seek to meet him.

Not merely in our own College at Delhi, but all over the Punjab,
the same new spirit of sacrifice was enkindled. During the time when
he lived a retired life of study in the Divinity School at Lahore, young
men, Christian and non-Christian, used to come to him for spiritual
help and counsel; and though at that time he was extremely reticent
and not altogether happy concerning the course he had chosen, the
silent influence of his example made its own deep impression. Gradually the news concerning him spread in wider circles, until he was
eagerly sought for to help at conventions for the deepening of spiritual
life all over the North of India. With regard to that portion of his
life, I have no personal memories to offer, for my own duties took me
to Santiniketan in Bengal, the home of Rabindranath Tagore, while
the Sadhu remained chiefly in the Punjab. Very occasionally, when I
went to the North, I would meet him; but our frequent intercourse,
which had been such a joy and blessing to me, came to an end after
I had left Delhi.

In those later years, right up to the time of his death, Principal
Rudra maintained his friendship with the Sadhu more closely than
ever, and he would often write to me about him. Now and then he
was perplexed by the strange narratives which the Sadhu had brought
back concerning his wanderings in Tibet, and he would often argue
with him that much of what he had experienced had been due to his
highly wrought imagination. He doubted some of the stories, but he
never doubted for a moment the sincerity and simplicity of the Sadhu
himself. That was beyond question.

After I had left Delhi, Lala Khub Ram, a science professor of St.
Stephen's College, often accompanied Principal Rudra to Kotgarh.
During their visits they had ample opportunities of meeting the Sadhu
and talking over these mysterious incidents with him, thus getting to
know more dearly his own point of view concerning the supernatural

world. While they differed from him in certain important respects, they both rejoiced to find that after his visits to the West, in 1920 and 1922, when he had become world-famous, his love for Christ had grown still deeper than before, and his humility had become more profound than ever. He had also ceased to speak in public about what he had seen in ecstatic visions, and confined himself to the simplest Gospel message.

Susil Rudra passed away in August, 1924. He suffered from a long and painful illness, very patiently borne, wherein his courageous bearing of pain seemed to make him gentler than ever. He was at Solan when the end came, in the midst of those same Simla Hills which he had learnt to love. While his outward strength was failing him, he prayed every day with earnest longing for a revival in the Indian Christian Church which would bring with it a renewed devotion to the service of Christ among the suffering. All through these last days I was able to be with him, and it was touching to witness how this longing increased while his bodily strength decayed.

Rudra's grave is in the Himalayan Hills, and it would now seem almost certain that the Sadhu also met his death in the recesses of the Himalayas. To both of them the one passion of their lives, which carried them through every humiliation, was the love of Christ. If they have been able to implant this in the hearts of the young Indian Christians, who looked up to them for guidance and example, they will not have lived in vain.

Chapter VIII

The Way of the Cross

No one was ever more dear to me in India than Susil Rudra, and no one helped me more to obtain a clear vision of the possibilities of the Christian faith in action. He showed me also, with great tenderness and sorrow, the failure of the Indian Church to set forward Christ's message in its true light, and the need of a new interpretation.

His last words to me, after we had received the sacrament together, were full of courage and hope. He saw before him with his dying eyes "a glorious Church, not having spot or wrinkle or any such thing: holy and without blemish."*

While he had been with me, as my loved companion, in earlier days at Kotgarh, he had written for English readers a remarkable pamphlet, which gave expression to his highest thoughts about Christ and His Church. He returned to these thoughts during his last illness before he became unconscious. They represented the tried and tested principles of his whole life.

"To distracted India,"** he had written in his pamphlet, "with its whole head and heart sick, there has come a message of hope... of a

---

* Ephesians 5:27
** See Renaissance in India, p. 248.

living Person, Jesus Christ, who declares: I am He that liveth and was dead, and behold I am alive for evermore.' That living Person in the plentitude of spiritual power embodies in Himself all the moral forces which go to create a vital and progressive organism—an organism which may find its goal in a united and independent nation. He embodies them, not merely as the Teacher, but as Himself the living motive Power behind them—the Power who gives new moral life to those who come to Him."

Susil Rudra was a patriot of a very high order, who loved India with a surpassing love. He wrote the words I have quoted at a time when he was in almost daily touch with Sadhu Sundar Singh at Kotgarh. It was the high Christian standard, which Sundar so courageously represented, that enabled him to write with such faith concerning the future triumph of the Cross. "A great Indian Church," he added, "is needed to form a great Indian nation."

It was through Susil that I came to understand these deeper thoughts regarding the destiny of the Indian Church and the Indian people, which he and Sundar discussed together, hour after hour.

I had learnt to love Sundar for his own sake and for his great love of Christ, his Lord and Master; but it was through Susil that I learnt also to sympathize with all that he had suffered in carrying out his Christian purpose. For Susil could enter into those sufferings with a knowledge that was intimately personal. He had known in his own life that same desolation of spirit which Sundar had felt on the day when he had left home and kindred and all that he had to follow Christ.

Susil's father, Piyare Mohan Rudra, had been one of Dr. Duff's converts in Calcutta, who had suffered social ostracism in early days because he had followed his own conscience and accepted Christ as his Saviour. Thus Susil had known as a boy, in his own home, what it was to suffer the loss of all things for Christ's sake, and he could never forget that experience. Nevertheless, he had strictly observed his father's attitude of complete loyalty to the Hindu tradition, wherever it did not conflict with his loyalty to Christ. He had remained a "Hindu" in every way that was possible, while living as a full member of the Christian community.*

To carry this out in practice had meant a lifelong struggle, both for father and son. They had followed the way of the Cross, and had joyfully accepted humiliation without bitterness. Misunderstood often by Indian Christians themselves; misunderstood also by the Hindu community, which had cast them out, they had found in Christ Himself their great consolation.

Sundar had been called upon, all through his life as a Christian, to face this same stern issue; and it was the greatest joy to Principal Rudra to watch and admire his wonderful courage as he took the straight course forward without swerving either to the right hand or the left. For Sundar had followed instinctively the same way of the Cross which Susil and his father had trodden. He had never, in later years, attacked bitterly, as converts are too prone to do, the religion in which he had been brought up. Rather, he welcomed men of religious principle wherever he found them, and did not seek to engage in controversy with them. They saw, in their turn, through his eyes, the love of Christ, and "took knowledge of him that he had been with Jesus." Like his own Master, he sought to build up rather than to pull down; to fulfil rather than to destroy; to be silent under rebuke; to bear humiliation with thankfulness; to testify by his life rather than by his words.

It was this patient, silent witness which won at last his father to confess Christ.

While I lived with Susil at Delhi, sharing his home with him, the Sadhu's name used to be constantly on our lips and his way of life discussed. The whole future of the Christian faith in India seemed to centre in the ideal he put before us. Could it be accepted by the Church in the Punjab, or would it be rejected? Were our own lives—we asked each other—helping or hindering? There could be no doubt

* The word "Hindu" carries with it a social as well as a religious significance.

what our own hearts desired; but were we carrying forward that desire to its fulfilment? My mind continually misgave me when I put this last question to myself.

Susil regretted all his life that he had gone too far in making one slight change, when he was quite young, in his outward habits. He had adopted European dress, as most Indian Christians had done. Thus, he had cut himself off, in this one respect, from his own past. On College feast days, however, and other important occasions, he would always wear his own Indian costume. But as soon as the function was over, he would go back to his drab European dress once more. Only one thing he would never abandon—his peculiar Indian head-dress. He dung to that to the end!

When I used to rally him about this, he would answer me with a disarming smile. "Don't insist, Charlie," he would say, half laughing, "or ask me to change my ways now. I'm too old to do that."

All the more, he admired the Sadhu for never having abandoned his national dress, even when he went to Europe. "I wish I had had the courage," he would say, "to do that. But it's too late to begin all over again."

This small feature of dress may appear to be of very slight importance. In itself, of course, it meant nothing. "The Kingdom of Heaven," says St. Paul, "is not meat and drink, but righteousness and peace and joy in the Holy Ghost." Nevertheless, as a symbol, it represented a cleavage between two incompatible ways of life; and this inner struggle was continually going on in Indian Christian lives, dividing their allegiance. Could the Christian faith become thoroughly akin to Indian conditions without losing its Christian character? That was the one vital question which was uppermost in earnest people's minds during those days.

Sadhu Sundar Singh, more than anyone else, helped to solve the problem in the right way. He boldly answered that Christ could walk along the Indian road and find there His companions and followers and friends. He believed that Christ could be truly found in India, if only Christians themselves did not obscure His presence. This simple faith in Christ, as the living Lord and Saviour, he held fast in his own heart and soul. He did not wish to define this faith in formal words, or to bind it to any particular outward organization. But he proved its power in his own life. He made no weak compromises. The salt in him did not lose its savour. And yet, at the same time, he remained "Indian" through and through, both in his outward dress and habits and in his thinking and creative mind.

Though his parables were drawn from his own experiences in India, they have won acceptance in every land because they tell of the living Christ. By continuing to be in every respect just what he was by his birth, a simple-minded Indian from an Indian village, he won everyone's heart, and carried more conviction than if he had tried to make himself Western. Even his halting use of the English language brought home more clearly his meaning, because it was natural and sincere. In the same way, all his Christian thoughts took an Eastern colour directly he gave them utterance; but they remained, even on that account, more close to the teaching of the Master.

"In the history of religion," writes Archbishop Soderblom, "Sundar is the first to show the whole world how the Gospel of Jesus Christ is reflected in unchanged purity in an Indian soul. Sundar answers a question we have ourselves asked: 'What will the Christianity of India be like, if it is to be anything at all but a "colony"?'

"Here is an Indian soul, who has remained as genuinely Indian as possible, in the best meaning of the word, while becoming absorbed in the love of Christ and completely accepting the Gospel. It would not be easy to find anyone, even in the West, who has more thoroughly assimilated the Gospel to himself than Sundar Singh. What is typical about him is not a fusion of Christianity and Hinduism, but a fresh presentation of Biblical Christianity that is in many ways stimulating and illuminating for ourselves."

Along many different channels this long process of bringing the Christian faith into direct touch with the religious genius of India is now being carried forward. Already its effect is made evident in many Churches. It is marked by the gradual disuse of alien forms of worship and the desire to abandon denominational differences. A return to the simplicity of Indian ways of living has also begun.

"If Christ," writes Principal Rudra, "becomes the object of the contemplation and love of India, who can place any limit to the assimilation of His life and spirit? And if Christ's spirit is assimilated, who can estimate its individual, social and political effects?"

Since Sadhu Sundar Singh set the example in faithfully following the way of the Cross, this transformation of the Indian Church from a foreign to an indigenous development has proceeded—in some parts of India very slowly, in other parts more rapidly. Ashrams* have sprung up among Indian Christians, along with brotherhoods of lowly service of the poor. The true Eastern setting of the Gospel has been made apparent. Much of the strangeness of the West has been taken away from the portrait of our Lord. Indian disciples are learning to walk closely in the steps which He trod.

Christian literature, art, music and architecture, which are more in touch with India and her people, are slowly taking their place in the life of the nation. Groups of villages, which are altogether Christian, are uniting to form a social and religious unit in the new civilization of the East. The renaissance of India is permeated more and more with Christian ideas. Christ's name and character are held in reverence far beyond the boundaries of the Church, and those who neither profess nor call themselves Christians are all unconsciously seeking to carry out His purpose.

It is not within the scope of a personal memoir, such as this, to dwell at length on the Sadhu's different journeys to the Far East, and also to America, Australasia, and Europe. My own recollections are confined to his life in India itself, and therefore I have no personal records of those travels in other lands. But I have gathered from the vivid and intimate memories of many friends that the impression he

---

*   Places of religious retreat.

left behind him went very deep indeed. He did not take the broad and easy path of speaking smooth things. Rather, he took the hard and narrow way of the Cross, and spoke the truth to the West in love. He became more and more a prophet, as he saw the luxury of Europe and America and contrasted it with the poverty of India. For his two visits to Christian lands brought with them a bitter disappointment.

He had expected to see the Spirit of Christ transforming the Western nations, but he found everywhere "comfort, money, luxury, and the things of the world." He had hoped to come into close touch with a life of Christian prayer and devotion, but he found instead noise and frantic haste which left no time for meditation. Like Tennyson, he compared man's life without prayer to an animal existence. "Men in the West," he said, "are so busy, that they have left prayer out of their lives altogether."

It is true that he met many devoted followers of Christ in these so-called Christian lands. "The noblest Christians," he said, "can be found in the West as well as in the East, and I long to sit at their feet." But he spoke with the severity of an Old Testament prophet concerning the evils of the West.

"In the Day of Judgment," he said with solemn warning, "non-Christians will receive a lighter sentence because they have not heard of Christ: but those in Christian lands will be punished more severely, because they have heard His message and have rejected it. Here, in the West, I see everywhere people who seem to think about nothing but pleasure, money and material comfort. I know that what I am saying will not please you; but I must obey my conscience and give you the message I have received from God."

Many were offended by this plain speaking from a young man, hardly more than thirty years old, coming to address them in broken English and dressed in a strange Eastern garb. Those who had come from mere curiosity, expecting to hear wonderful stories, went away disappointed, but many took heed of what he said in such an unconventional manner.

"This is the last time you will ever see me," he said with sadness at the end of his travels in the West. On that very account, he had felt all the more bound in spirit to deliver the message which the Lord had given him to utter.

In contrast with this outward severity, we may take some sentences from a letter written to me by Dr. Karl Fries, of Sweden, who had welcomed him to his own home. "Never," writes Karl Fries, "did we hear from him a harsh word, or an unkind judgment, while he was our guest. He was, in every detail, a true Christian gentleman. Much of his time was spent alone, in his room, engaged in prayer. He looked at things always from the spiritual side and was more eager for the beauties of Nature than the works of man."

Dr. Frank N. D. Buchman, the founder of the Oxford Group Movement, who was with him in America, gave me the same picture of his life of prayer maintained amid all the multiple engagements of a Western tour.

Sundar Singh always spoke with an admiration and affection, deeply touching to hear, of those missionaries to whom, in God's providence, he owed so much. For men and women such as these, who were the salt of the earth, his gratitude was unbounded.

Chapter IX

In His Steps

W E come now to one characteristic feature of Sadhu Sundar Singh's life, which seemed to overrule his actions and shape the course he took in a singular manner. With a childlike simplicity, he sought step by step to follow literally the example of his Lord and Saviour Jesus Christ.

The Gospels, in their Urdu translation, were his Bible. He carried a small New Testament about with him wherever he went. For many years of his life it was the one book he studied, and he gave it his own inter-

SCRIPTURE TESTIMONY
Scriptures essential for knowing and loving God
2 TIMOTHY 3:14-17
· HEBREWS 4:12

pretation as he meditated upon it. Above all, he read its text in the light of that supreme moment when he saw Christ face to face and became His disciple. I used to watch him at Kotgarh studying his Gospel in Urdu with deep attention, and he would speak about the joy it gave him. One of the last letters he wrote, early in April, 1929, before he went on that journey into Tibet, from which he never returned, was to the Bible Society in England, testifying what untold spiritual wealth he had found in this most precious treasure he possessed.

To Sundar Singh, in those years when I knew him best, there was an all-inclusive article of the Christian Faith. Christ was to him, in his own spiritual life, the living image of the invisible God. He saw God in the face of Jesus Christ. He did not come to the idea of God through the Old Testament; for he only rarely studied in detail the Psalms and the Prophets. The Gospels were all in all to him. He knew the Gospel story of the Lord Jesus Christ by heart; it lived in his memory and fashioned his daily thoughts.

In his book of visions, the Sadhu gives us the picture of what was made clear to him about "seeing God." He writes: "A few months ago I was lying alone in my room suffering acutely from an ulcer in my eye. The pain was so great that I could do no other work, so I spent the time in prayer and intercession. One day I had been thus engaged for only a few minutes when the spiritual world was opened to me and I found myself surrounded by numbers of angels. Immediately I forgot all my pain.... I asked: 'Do the angels and saints always look upon the face of God, and if they see Him in what form does He appear?'

"One of the saints said: 'As the sea is full of water, so is the whole universe filled with God.... Because He is infinite, His children, who are finite, can see Him only in the form of Christ.'"

What Sundar Singh thus saw and heard in this vision has a background of Indian religious thought behind it; for the simile of the ocean, as a picture of the Divine Life, is common to all Indian literature; and the thought of the Formless One taking Form, in order to make Himself known to mankind, is common also.*

Christ had revealed to Sundar Singh the fullness of the Divine Life. He had brought God near to him in a human form. Therefore every detail of that character of the Master was studied by the disciple with intense and rapt devotion. To most Christians the Old Testament background has afforded a long training and discipline concerning the

---

* See What I Owe to Christ, Chap. V.

holiness and righteousness of God before His name of Love is revealed. But with Sundar Singh, this background was lacking. He leapt at once from the vague belief concerning God, which he had inherited from his mother, to the New Testament, wherein God's nature of perfect love is the crown of revelation. It is quite possible that his character lacked something by never having had this discipline. But at the same time it saved him from crudities which have hardly yet been thrown off among ourselves.

His one passionate desire, year after year, when we met him at Kotgarh, was to make an immediate pilgrimage, in some way or other, to the Holy Land, and there walk along the very road where Christ had walked, and pray on the Mount of Olives at the very spot where Christ had prayed. Even as early as 1908 he had found his way to Bombay, hoping to get a passage to Port Said on some cargo boat, and thus go forward to the Holy Land, but he was unable to do so. His visit to the West, in 1920, which opened every country in the world to him, was originally due to this intense longing to go to Palestine. He found that it was impossible to obtain in India a passport directly after the Great War, and someone told him that he could obtain one more easily if he went to England. That information immediately set his mind working. At last he determined to make a journey direct to England, hoping afterwards to reach the Holy Land from thence.

When he set foot in Palestine at last, in the year 1922, his highly sensitive nature was stirred to its very depths. He walked each step of the sacred way with such intentness of emotion that he seemed to be dwelling there with his Master, and feeling His presence intimately near wherever he went.

We are always coming across these literal "imitations" in the Sadhu's own life. Indeed he was often too literal; but his devotion was so great that he could not go far astray. With his vivid imagination he saw everything, even in his daily life, through pictures of the mind. This made each saying of Christ so living to him, that he longed to follow in his Master's steps by literal obedience to His word.

When Jesus said: "Foxes have holes and the birds of the air have nests, but the Son of Man hath not where to lay His head," Sundar Singh took this at once as sanctioning the Sadhu life. When Jesus said: "Take neither purse nor scrip neither two coats," he obeyed to the very letter

In the light of this literal tendency in the Sadhu's imaginative life, it is possible to appreciate the significance of the step which he took early in 1913. For he put into practice a desire which had long been in his heart unfulfilled. He went out into the wilderness to keep a fast, just as Jesus his Master did, under the open sky, without any protection from the wild beasts.

He retired alone, into the jungle between Hardwar and Dehra Dun, and gave himself up to prayer and meditation while his strength and consciousness lasted. He intended, if his body could endure the strain, to fast for the same period as his Lord, but he broke down after a few days.

He tells us that one of the reasons for undertaking this fast was to find out whether the inner peace, which he enjoyed as a Christian, was quite independent of the body and remained a thing apart, or whether it was bound up with the body and changed with its changing emotions.

"Before I attempted the fast," he said, "I was assailed by temptations. More especially when I was tired I used to get annoyed when people came to talk to me and ask questions. I still feel this difficulty, but nothing like so much as before.... Before the fast, I suffered also from other temptations. When suffering from hunger and thirst I used to complain and to ask why the Lord did not provide. He had told me not to take any money with me. If I had taken money I could have bought what I needed. Since the fast, however, when overtaken by physical hardships, I say: 'It is my Father's will; perhaps I have done something to deserve it.' Again, before the fast I was sometimes tempted to give up the life of a Sadhu with its hardships and go back to the luxury of my father's house, to get married and live in comfort. Could I not be a good Christian and live a life of communion with God there also?

But I saw that, though it was no sin for others to live in comfort and have money and home, God's call for me was different... My real marriage is with Christ."*

The effort he made terminated abruptly for his physical strength left him. He had not practised fasting of this kind before, and therefore the strain was excessive. Some wood-cutters found him in the jungle half-dead and brought him down to Rishikesh. He was taken to Dehra Dun and then to Annfield, where under the care of some Indian Christians he was nursed back to health.

Sundar Singh taught in parables. Here again his first thought in doing so was to follow literally in the footsteps of his Master. As Christ went about the villages of Galilee, so he himself went

SCRIPTURE TESTIMONY
Jesus taught many things through parables
MARK 4:2

about the villages in the Punjab and in the Simla Hills. As Christ taught the country-folk in simple parables, so he would use the homeliest illustrations from the life of the country-side. Even when he came to the West, he still kept his manner of speech.

The stories which he told showed remarkable powers of observation, and the points he made in them were so convincing that when once they were heard they could never be forgotten. Some of his most vivid illustrations were taken from what he saw in the Simla Hills.

"In 1921," he relates, "there broke out a jungle fire in the Himalayas. While most of the people around were busy in putting it out, I noticed several men standing and looking fixedly into a tree. 'What are you looking at?' I asked. They, in reply, pointed to a nest full of young birds on the tree whose branches were already burning. Above it, a bird was flying about in great distress. They said: 'We wish we could save that nest, but we cannot go near because of the blazing fire.' A few minutes later the nest caught fire, and I thought: 'Now the motherbird will fly away.' Instead, to my great astonishment, I saw her fly down

---

* Streeter & Appasamy. *The Message of Sadhu Sundar Singh*, pp. 23 f.

and spread her wings over the young ones. In a few minutes the poor bird was burnt to ashes along with her youngsters. I had never seen anything like it before, and said to those standing near: 'Are we not astonished at this wonderful love? Think how much more wonderful must be the love of Him who has created such an unselfish love in His creatures. The same infinite and unselfish love brought Jesus Christ down from heaven into this world to become man that, by giving His own life, He might save us who were dying in our sins.'"

One further instance may be given from the imagery of the Himalayas:

"Till the sun's heat," he writes, "has melted the snow of the mountain tops, it cannot flow down and irrigate the sun-dried and thirsty plain. Until the snow is melted it cannot be drawn as water vapour to form clouds, from which it can come down as rain to make the parched and thirsty land green and fruitful. If we are not melted by the rays of the Sun of Righteousness, and by the fire of the Holy Spirit, we can neither quench the thirst of any famished soul nor bring him to the Fountain of Life, where he will be satisfied and live forever. May God give us grace so to live Christ in our daily lives that we may be instrumental in bringing others to our Saviour."

Among his illustrations, none stand out more clearly in their freshness than those which he derived from his visit with Sir W. Willcocks to Palestine in 1922, to which reference has already been made. They reveal how his heart and soul were continually with the Lord and Master whom he served.

SCRIPTURE TESTIMONY
Whoever hears and believes has eternal life
JOHN 5:24 · ROMANS 10:9-17

"In 1922," he writes, "with a friend, I was greatly refreshed by drinking the sweet and soothing water of a famous well. An hour or two later I was again thirsty, and those words of our Lord came forcibly to my mind: 'Whosoever drinketh of this water shall thirst again; but whosoever drinketh of the water that I shall give him shall never thirst, but the water that I shall give him shall be in him a well of water springing up into everlasting life.'

"I had just drunk of a well that men had dug and was again thirsty. In all humility and thankfulness I can say that since I gave my heart to Christ and drank of that water which He gave me, I have never been thirsty, because He is indeed the Fountain of Life."

The Mount of Olives, the place of the Holy Sepulchre, the Way to Calvary—all these sacred places filled his mind day and night. They gave him also some of his most graphic illustrations.

"Many Christians," he said, "are like Mary at the Sepulchre, who loved Jesus and went to see Him in His grave when He was already risen from the dead. She loved Jesus with her whole heart, and yet when she saw Him outside the tomb she did not recognize Him. Her sight was blinded with tears. It was as if there were a mist before her eyes which prevented her from seeing Him. It is the same with many Christians. They love Jesus without seeing in Him the Saviour who is risen from the dead—the living Christ. They cannot see Him on account of the mists of sin and error: their eyes are blinded with tears of sorrow. But when they open their hearts fully to Him, then they recognize Him."

One more parable was probably suggested to him by those who took him through the Holy Land. It points out how the Sea of Galilee which takes in the pure fresh water from the snows of Lebanon remains always fresh and sweet, with the flowers of the field covering its rising banks, because it always passes on the water it receives. But the Dead Sea, which receives the same water that has flowed through the Sea of Galilee, turns the pure fresh water into salt water so full of brine that on its banks nothing can grow at all. It is a Dead Sea because it takes in but never gives out. So Christians who unselfishly pass on the good gifts which God gives to them remain pure and fresh in their spiritual life, while those who take in God's gifts and never give out unselfishly to others, become dead and lifeless. They not only ruin their own lives, but also the lives of those around who depend on them for spiritual help.

Those who heard him speak about the Holy Land in India after his return can never forget the gleam of light which came into his eyes, and the rapt look upon his face. He told his story almost like one in a dream. The things in Palestine that jar on the sensitive mind to-day—the crowds of sight-seeing tourists, the rivalries of religious sects, the rush of the motor traffic and the vulgarizing of human life—all these seemed to leave no sad impression behind them, because he dwelt in spirit so entirely with his Lord. The Living Christ was by his side and he was conscious of His presence.

The one Book that revealed Christ to him as he walked in these sacred paths was the Bible. Every page of it became illuminated and more dear to him than ever it had been before, after this visit to the Holy Land. His vivid imagination was enkindled by its stories, and its pages became still more living to him.

"The Bible," he said, "is the Book of books, because it is the Book of God. It is my Guide and Light, and Food for my soul. Experience has proved the fact that there is no other book in the world beside this, which can meet the spiritual needs of men. It is now about a quarter of a century since this precious Book introduced me to its Author; and all this time I have found my Saviour to be exactly the same as recorded in this Book. He has been to me all that we read concerning Him there. Language difficulties and textual criticism have not hidden its truths nor hindered in the least its life-giving influence in my heart, because of these words—'They are spirit and they are life.'

"In reading the Bible, I have found untold and eternal wealth of riches, such as I never thought nor dreamt before; and now in passing on its message to others, and sharing it with them, its blessing to me and to them continually increases. People can see the Book and its readers, but its wonderful unseen power and force of attraction are only known by those who read it sincerely and prayerfully. Just as the magnet and needle can be seen, but the magnetic force which draws the needle to itself is hidden and unseen, so the unseen power of this Word of God draws sinners like me to the Saviour."*

When I asked Willie Hindle to give his own explanation why Sundar seemed to me so sad when I met him at Simla in 1926, he said that this thought of death was ever present with the Sadhu after he had passed the allotted span of years that Christ had lived. A sadness had grown upon him when the Lord delayed His "coming."

Each journey that he took towards Tibet in those later years was an adventure upon which he set out with the anticipation that he might meet death. He never fully expected to return. The love of Christ constrained him, and whether he was fit for the journey or unfit he pressed on. The vision of his youth remained even after some of its splendour had faded.

Sundar, all through those days of his early manhood, had a flaming passion—partly derived from his mother's teaching about the Sikh Gurus and partly from his visions of Christ. It was to follow his Saviour even unto death. This had been always in his mind throughout those years of suffering on his journeys to and from Tibet, where Christ was his sole Companion. He had come to a strangely literal expectation that he would meet his own death at the very same age of life at which his Lord had been crucified. Therefore he had looked forward to dying at the age of thirty-three. He did not speak of this in public, but only to those who were his closest friends. The thought of it had gripped his imagination, especially during his journey to the Holy Land, where he had meditated so intensely upon the Death and Passion of his Saviour. After he had passed through the thirty-fourth year of his life, and his own death was delayed, he was disappointed.

---

* Address given at the British and Foreign Bible Society, London.

Chapter X

The World of Spirit

THIS chapter will be more difficult to write than any other because the village life of India, with its medieval outlook, is unfamiliar to the modern West. Sundar Singh retained that "medieval" mind all through the years when my recollections of him were most vivid. It was his great strength among his own village people; and yet it had its weakness also. It led to an almost credulous acceptance of the miraculous. At the same time, it kept his imagination fresh and young all through the years of manhood which followed his conversion. It therefore enabled him to undertake adventures in the spiritual sphere, which would never have been possible without the recklessness of childlike faith.

We moderns have *our* strength also. We are more severely critical of superstition than any other age in human history. Thereby, we have emancipated ourselves from many haunting fears. But, side by side with this, we have a paralysing weakness, of which we are often almost unaware. For in the crowded rush of modern city life, in the midst of ever-speeding traffic, we have tended to lose touch with the deeper spiritual realities which underlie the universe. Wordsworth, more than a century ago, made us realize this danger in lines which have become commonplace and yet they carry with them to-day an even more serious warning than ever before. He speaks to us of the obsession of the outer world:

> "...*late and soon,*
> *Getting and spending, we lay waste our powers:*
> *Little we see in Nature that is ours:*
> *We have given our hearts away, a sordid boon."*

He tells us how, for all the finer notes, we have no ear: we are out of tune.

The consequence of this has been, that the best part of us has become cruelly neglected; and every now and then Nature herself cries out in agony. She will not allow us to lose the better part of human existence.

In the simple village life of India, though there are many glaring evils and gross credulities, this child-imagination has not been cast aside as a thing outworn. It is amazingly active. Fancy still plays her wonderful part in creating its own picture language for the human spirit. Village children, as they go forward on life's journey from childhood to old age, do not desert the realm of wonder, or content themselves with the dull commonplace. Marvels in Nature and in human life fill their waking thoughts, and meet them face to face in their dreams.

Granted that evil spirit-forces are at work as well as good. Nevertheless, at least imagination has its wings to soar, and man's daily vision is not bounded by the material sense of animal needs. For the humblest villager, who lives on scanty fare, will spend every coin he has put by, and mortgage his whole future, in order to make a pilgrimage to Mount Kailash amid the snows; or to bathe in the sacred waters of the Ganges at Benares; or to reach by weary marches the great Temple at Puri on the shore of the Bay of Bengal. The rapt look on the faces of these village pilgrims, as they go forward singing on their way, declares plainly that "man does not live by bread alone."

Among the interior regions of the Himalayas, and all along the borders of Tibet, this inner sense of a mysterious Spirit-Universe, enveloping the material world of outward things and intermingling with the hidden powers of Nature herself, becomes vividly intense among travellers who have spent long years there. They have felt suddenly descending upon them an awe of the supernatural, difficult to describe in words.

While this peculiar intensity of awe is experienced in the high mountains, the same feeling exists, in a lesser degree, over every part of rural India in the plains. This village life is intimately known to me through long familiarity with its people. Hour after hour I have listened to the talk in the evening, when strange happenings among the "spirit-folk" have been eagerly canvassed and discussed. Such stories are rarely challenged by those who are sitting round the *huqqa* "listening in." For there is always a ready will to believe.

In the dusk of the evening twilight, dim shapes are seen and faint voices are heard. The air itself, along certain paths, seems haunted by spirit forms. This spirit-world is felt by the villagers nearly all day long. Some of the more thoughtful of them will sit for long hours in silence during the midday heat half-dreaming about it. Others will brood over it while working in the fields and offer up a prayer to God for guidance and protection. Solitude is easily obtained by those who may wish to keep it. Not seldom a solitary singer will go on singing his song to God far into the night, or else at break of dawn.

Amid such surroundings as these, in the village of Rampur, Sundar Singh was born and had his home. From his earliest childhood, the daily instructions he received from the Hindu Scriptures brought before his singularly receptive mind incredibly romantic legends about divine heroes who performed wonderful deeds and lived miraculous lives. The stories of the Sikh martyrs were also replete with glowing incidents of noble endurance. His own daily life, in the large household of Sardar Sher Singh, his father, stimulated his thoughts in these directions. For all the members of the family, including his own mother, believed in the supernatural with heart and soul. They would therefore encourage the young lad's eagerness to penetrate into those mysterious things which were of absorbing interest to themselves. Neither he, nor they, had yet come into such close contact with modern critical thought as to raise any doubt or question about the validity of what their forefathers had told them.

It is with no sense of disparagement that I have brought forward this aspect of Indian village life. Indeed, in my own home in England, when I was a boy, we lived in a world all day long that was full of the Book of Revelation; and my father and mother never left it.* The supernatural thus became natural to me, just as it is natural to-day in village India.

When Sundar Singh became a Christian this innate love of the marvellous was in no way diminished. The extraordinary character of his own conversion led him directly to that inner kingdom of the soul where miracles are of daily occurrence, and the line which divides the outward from the inward becomes almost invisible. In his Urdu New Testament, he used to read concerning the wonderful deeds of Christ described in the Gospels. The Acts of the Apostles showed to him the very same deeds continuing in the early Church. Therefore, as he went forward step by step in his discipleship, seeking humbly to follow Christ, he passed into a world of new Christian experiences, which corresponded in some degree with the miraculous world of imagination he had inhabited before. The object of his worship was Christ: the supernatural character of events remained the same.

Sundar Singh had, from the very first, powers of imagination and mystical vision far beyond those of ordinary people. He could see things that others could not see, and lived in a world of his own. It was very noticeable how he had retained, long after childhood, the power of visualizing things he saw inwardly with the mind. Wordsworth tells us how he himself, as a poet, spent three days on Salisbury Plain and was haunted by visions of the past. Sundar had the same poetic

---

*   See *What I Owe to Christ*, Chaps. III and IV.

nature very highly developed. His visualizing faculty grew with him as he lived among the mountains; and I have often wondered whether life in the high mountain air, amid the solitudes of Nature, enhances such a disposition. Among the Highlands of Scotland, for instance, and in the West of Ireland, where the wild aspect of Nature has not yet entirely disappeared, the people themselves seem to retain powers which are lost to ordinary city folk.

During the long solitary journeys which Sundar took, year after year, in the Himalayas, these creative powers of his own imagination had full play. Like some new opening scene in the great drama of the Apocalypse, the Holy City would seem to be about to "descend out of heaven, from God." No wonder he held fast to a literal "Second Coming" in the clouds of heaven of the Son of Man and would have nothing to do with those who spiritualized away the literal words. One of his favourite texts was taken from the Book of Revelation, where the prophet writes: "Behold he cometh with clouds, and every eye shall see him; and they also which pierced him."

Not only inwardly, but also outwardly, during these adventurous journeys, he seemed to be moving in a world of spirit. His passion for solitude and his practice of trance-like moods evidently increased this initial childhood's difficulty of distinguishing fact from imaginative vision. For the more he lived in the midst of Nature, with her haunting voices, and became one of her favoured children, the more extraordinary his spiritual experiences became. During a period of years while he was still young, he spoke openly about these with a freedom that he afterwards regretted. For he found that men and women turned to him as a marvel-worker and did not turn to Christ. The discovery of this made him much more reticent, until at last he ceased to speak about such abnormal incidents altogether.

One of the miraculous stories about which he had spoken often in private, during his first visit to the West, was concerning the marvellous Maharishi of Kailash, who had lived an unbelievable number of years, in a cave, as a Christian hermit. Sundar Singh was convinced that he had actually met and also spoken with this hermit, on certain definite occasions. But the conversations, which he reported afterwards? seem to have been derived from his own ecstatic trances. A book of translations of these was published in India without his authority, which is obviously visionary in character.*

That the Sadhu himself had doubts concerning these happenings becomes clear from one fact which has not yet been recorded. When he was in the South of England, with Willie Hindle, he insisted on going over to France; and for a whole day he made a search up and down a poor quarter of Paris, but failed to find what he wanted. At the end of the day, he told his English friend that the Maharishi had described to him a poor girl's home in Paris and he wished to verify this, but had not been able to do so.**

One day, in London, some persons of high rank in society were invited to meet him. But when he found that they had gathered together merely to hear from him about the Maharishi, he refused pointblank to speak about him. "I came," he said sternly, "not to speak about the Rishi, but about Christ." When he entered the room his presence as a prophet could be felt. There was an awed silence, and he brought those who had come out of curiosity down on their knees to prayer.

His eyes were always set upon Christ. Anything that prevented his dear witness to his Master he swept out of the way. Once, in Ceylon, he had healed a child, on whom he had laid his hands. But when he found that his fame had gone abroad as a miracle-worker, and attention was being drawn to himself rather than to Christ, his Master, he stopped at once. Just when his own fame was at its height, and the report was spreading like wildfire that a new wonder-worker had arrived, he went away from the place. "Pray to Christ," he said, "for healing. He is the Healer. My message is to speak of Christ." Those who were constantly with him, in the later years of his life, have told me that this refusal to speak about wonders became more and more

*   *Saved to Serve*, translated by Alfred Zahir.
**   This vision about Paris is referred to in *Saved to Serve*.

his settled mood. He would gladly speak about his own conversion and his own repentance, but would say nothing about the marvels which had happened to him afterwards. He thus put into practice the great word of the Apostle: "God forbid that I should glory, save in the name of our Lord Jesus Christ, by whom the world is crucified unto me and I unto the world."

Those who may wish to know what he gave out to the world concerning these marvels may find them in the biographies.* In this memoir, I would only bring forward two simple illustrations which have come within the range of my own experience. They appear to me to bear the hall-mark of truth upon them and to throw light upon the Sadhu's remarkable personality. For this reason, I feel that they may be here recorded.

The former of these stories is told by one who writes that he met the Sadhu travelling on the B.B. and C.I. Railway. A man, with magical powers, was in the compartment and had mesmerized one of those present who had come under his evil eye. This led the Sadhu to interfere, and the magician immediately began to try to mesmerize Sundar Singh himself.

"The latter"—so the one who tells the story relates—"hung down his head and busied himself in offering prayer to God. The wizard tried for half an hour to influence the Sadhu himself with his charms and incantations, but he could not succeed. Whereupon he suddenly cried out that the Sadhu had a book in his pocket, and unless he parted with it, his charms would be of no avail. The Sadhu had a copy of St. John's Gospel which he instantaneously took out and put on the bench. Again the wizard tried but failed. Then he cried out that still there was a page of the same book in the Sadhu's pocket. This page he had picked up from the road out of reverence for it, and he took it out, on the wish of the wizard, and placed it beside the book. The wizard again tried, but with no result. Then he asked the Sadhu to take off his cloak, and he obeyed him. Again the wizard tried, but finally

---

* See Notes, p. 204.

gave up, saying that he had found a mysterious power pervading him. Then the Sadhu told the wizard to accept Christ as his Guru, whose power he saw within him and against whose power the evil spirits were powerless."

Behind a narrative like this there was a real occurrence. One could be certain that Sundar Singh, as a Christian, would have taken exactly this attitude towards any attempt to mesmerize him by some magical process. But whether the story is correctly reported in detail, one cannot be certain; for, even from an eye-witness, there are not unlikely to be minor additions.

To Sundar Singh, as I knew him, the whole scene would have meant a "life and death" struggle between the powers of light and the powers of darkness. It would remind him of the Acts of the Apostles, how Elymas the sorcerer had sought to defeat Barnabas and Saul by his sorcery, and to turn Sergius Paulus from the faith.*

The second incident happened in Bareri, near to Kotgarh, and was told me by one of my own pupils of St. Stephen's College, Delhi. He had also written about it in a book.**

SCRIPTURE TESTIMONY
As we serve Him, the Lord will be our defense
LUKE 10:19 · 2 THESSALONIANS 3:1-3

"One night," he writes, "just before we went to bed, we noticed lights moving in the valley, and the Sadhu explained to me that men were probably in pursuit of a leopard.... Long after midnight I was aroused by a movement in the room. The Sadhu had risen from his bed and was moving towards the door, which opened on the wooden stairs outside the house. The creaking of the wood made it clear that he was going down. Knowing that the Sadhu spent hours of the night in prayer,' I was not surprised at this. But when half an hour or so had passed and he had not returned, I became uneasy: the thought of the leopard in the valley made me feel anxious. So I got out of bed, passed into

---

*   Acts 13:6-13
**   *More Yarns about India*, by Shoran Singha, Edinburgh House Press, London.

the dressing-room, and looked out of the window towards the forest. A few yards from the house I saw the Sadhu sitting looking down into the deep valley. It was a beautiful night. The stars were shining brightly; a light wind rustled the leaves of the trees. For a few moments I watched the silent figure of the Sadhu. Then my eyes were attracted by something moving on his right. An animal was coming towards him. As it got nearer I saw that it was a leopard. Choked with fear, I stood motionless near the window, unable even to call. Just then the Sadhu turned his face towards the animal and held out his hand. As though it had been a dog, the leopard lay down and stretched out its head to be stroked.

"It was a strange, unbelievable scene, and I can never forget it. A short time afterwards the Sadhu returned and was soon asleep, but I lay awake wondering what gave that man such power over wild animals."

This is Shoran Singha's story of what he actually saw that night. When I questioned him closely about it, he told me how he was so benumbed by fear that he could not even cry out. It all happened at a place in Bareri, which I know so well that I can still easily recall every detail to mind. Therefore, I have confidence that the incident occurred as Shoran has described it. He goes on to relate how in the morning he had asked the Sadhu: "Were you not frightened when you saw the leopard?"

"Why should the leopard harm me?" he replied. "I was not his enemy. Moreover, so long as I trust in Christ, I have no cause to tremble."

On another occasion, however, Sundar himself tells us that he was terrified. He woke up in a cave, where he had spent the night, and found a large leopard beside him. He confessed afterwards that for a moment he was almost paralysed with fear; for he was taken quite unawares. But, once outside the cave, his courage returned, and he gave thanks to God who had thus preserved his life.

Many occurrences, easily verifiable, have happened in India, where men of religion living alone in the jungle have been unharmed by the wild beasts. The same thing happened in medieval Europe. The account of the magician is also in no way strange to those who have moved about among the villages of India. How far other stories about the Sadhu in Tibet and Nepal and other inaccessible regions may be relied on can hardly be discussed within the compass of this book, which is a personal memoir only.

But the authentic records of mankind seemed clearly to point out how in the wild places of the earth and under the highest tension of the human spirit, voices are heard and sights are seen that could never be dreamt of in ordinary life. Therefore, if we are wise we shall keep an open mind about them. The closed view of the universe, that strangely prevailed last century, has already begun to give place to a wider horizon of scientific vision. This does not mean that we are to go back to credulity and superstition, but rather that we are to go forward admitting with true humility our present ignorance concerning the ultimate laws of the spiritual life.

The Sadhu evidently crossed and recrossed, times without number, the border between the dream-life and the waking-life, until the margin itself became blurred. He lived for hours together in an intermediate state. That is what his ecstasy or trance denoted. But to put the matter thus does not explain the secret of the hidden powers within the sold of man. For the same mysterious questionings concerning the soul's real life—whether "in the body or out of the body"—have vexed the wisest thinkers of the human race from earliest days. We have Plato's and Wordsworth's conceptions of a pre-existent state. We have Euripides with his famous couplet:

"Who knows if death be life, or life be death?"

We have the Chinese philosopher, who could not decide whether the dream-life was the true life of the soul or the active life in the world. We have also the common theory among Hindus and other religious men in the East with regard to the soul's wandering through many stages of existence.

All this speculation on the part of the wisest of men should make us pause, if we are ever inclined to reject at first sight evidence which comes to us concerning the unseen world of Spirit. We may even begin to have confidence that this mysterious universe will at last reveal to us some of her deepest secrets, and that even in this generation we may be on the eve of great discoveries, throwing light on many incidents of a miraculous character recorded in the Bible, and also on much that the Sadhu sincerely believed to be miraculous in his own experience.*

---

* In relation to this whole chapter, the words of G. Bernard Shaw's play, "St. Joan," should be remembered:

JOAN: I hear voices telling me what to do. They come from God.
ROBERT: They come from your imagination.
JOAN: Of course. This is how the messages of God come to us.

Chapter XI

The Sadhu

THE picture which I would wish to draw from memory of Sadhu Sundar Singh is difficult to outline in its true proportions. For while he was fundamentally simple, naïve and childlike, he was also surprisingly many-sided. Some new aspect of his character would suddenly appear which seemed to contradict first impressions.

Thus, although he had learnt through much suffering and self-denial a wonderful meekness and gentleness of spirit, he would occasionally become imperious when thwarted about some new proposal which his own inner guidance told him to be right. It was easy to see that, like Moses, he had learnt to be "the meekest of men" in a hard school. At times, when he felt he was right, he would sweep away all opposition in a forceful manner. This led to changes of plans when he was on a preaching tour—a habit disconcerting to the clock-like regularity of the West. In this respect he was a prophet and needed to be treated as a prophet. He had no conception at first as to the amount of trouble any change of plans caused in the West, and it was difficult to bring the fact home to him. Time-table regularity he abhorred. It seemed to be contrary to the freedom of the Spirit.

On one point he gave way immediately when its effect was pointed out to him. He had felt it a duty on landing in England to retain his simple Sadhu dress unchanged. His friends were anxious, on account of the damp cold of England, to modify this in two respects. They wished him to wear shoes with warm socks, and also an overcoat. At first he laughed at such precautions, saying that he was used to a much more severe climate in the Himalayas! But when it was pointed out that if he came inside the house with his Sadhu dress all damp from the rain, and his feet covered with mud, it would inconvenience his hostess, he at once gave way so far as to wear sandals and a cloak.

Typical incidents are told about him by one who acted as his secretary during his tour in Switzerland. The people in the mountains, seeing his feet only protected by sandals as he walked through the melting snow, pitied him, saying: "Pauvre homme, il doit avoir froid." But his feet were so hardened that he scarcely felt the cold. Once a Swiss mountaineer said to him: "Do not the stones cut your feet?" He replied with a joke: "My feet are so hard that they cut the stones!"

He was very sensitive with regard to the staring gaze of onlookers as he passed along the streets. On one occasion in Switzerland, his friends urged him to come out on the platform while the train was halting, but he was afraid that a crowd would gather. It was pointed out that there were only two or three people present, but he remained where he was. Again, later, in the Isle of Wight, he would walk up and down on a roof terrace of the house where Mrs. Parker was staying, but she could not induce him to go outside. He had been so disturbed by people staring at him that he would not face it unless he were obliged to do so. It is difficult for us to realize the agony of shyness which he felt in the midst of people so entirely different from those among whom he spent his life in the villages of the Punjab and amid the Simla Hills.

This sensitive nature made him feel acutely what was happening around him, especially if he himself were the unconscious cause of any pain. On one dark night of snow and rain in a Swiss village, he found that his hostess, in spite of her age, had come down to the railway station to welcome his arrival. On his way to her house he said to her: "I cannot tell you how sorry I am that you were put to such trouble for me. It hurts me when I make anyone suffer like that. Once, in India, when I was standing with a friend, and a stone, or a branch of a tree—I forget which—fell on his leg, I fainted, but he did not. He bore it better than I did."

Sundar Singh's courtesy to ladies, especially when they were old, was a pleasure to witness. *"Qu'il est poli!"* said one Swiss lady when she saw his courtesy. *"J'aime cet homme!"* In the hospital, when he passed through the little children's ward, the tiny patients whispered to the nursing sisters: *"C'est le Christ!"*

On his European tours he tried patiently to accommodate himself to the incessant rush and hurry of a crowded programme, but he broke down under it at last. After one hurried meeting, at which he had given an address, he spoke very little. He knew he had failed. "But the people listened very well," argued his host. "Yes," he replied, "but I had not got the victory over myself. They made me go straight from the dinner-table to the meeting. I was rushed from one to the other. It was not possible for me to say: 'No,' but I could not bear it. God is always quiet. He never makes a noise. His voice is a still, small voice."

One more slight sketch may be given from this secretary's note-book. "I have never seen," she writes towards the end, "such a beautiful face as Sundar Singh's at that time when he was praying. It was so wonderfully peaceful. I think others saw its beauty also, for all those who were near him could not take their eyes off him.... The next morning the Sadhu was at the breakfast-table. Mr. Steiger's dog was near him, for all animals go to him. When he was staying with Pastor L., the cat jumped on his knee. 'Just see,' he said, 'what love God puts into this little animal! How much more does he put in us.' He spoke of a very savage dog in India which was always quiet when it was near him."

Of all the countries he visited abroad, Switzerland came nearest to his heart. It reminded him daily of his own Himalayas, which rise up from the valleys on a still vaster scale of grandeur than the Alps. He

loved best of all the Swiss village people, who flocked in to see him
from the remote recesses of the mountains; for he seemed to be far
more at home with them than with the crowds in the great cities in
Northern Europe.

While he was travelling in Malaya, China and Japan, he showed
the same deep affection for the simple village folk. The reason for this
was that he himself was a villager, both by his birth and upbringing.
His active life also, in India, was spent more in the villages than in
the towns. In South India, in Travancore, it was a peculiar happiness
to him to find the whole country-side marked by Christian churches,
where the Syrian Christians had long ago been settled on the land.
Frequently, in his letters, he mentions the Annual Convention of this
ancient Church, where more than thirty thousand assemble in one
place to hear the Word of God. These Syrian Christians, he asserts,
have kept the true simplicity of the Gospel. They take no thought
either of food or raiment, but hunger for the Bread of Life.

The whole setting of this vast Convention in South India profoundly
moved his heart by its simple longing for Christ's message. It brought
vividly before him the narrative of the Gospel, where Jesus had compas-
sion on the multitude because they fainted and were scattered abroad "as
sheep having no shepherd." Yet they continued to cling to the Saviour
in order to "hear the gracious words that proceeded out of His mouth."

"Our Lord," he said with feeling, "loved the country people best.
He called them His own 'sheep.' He would never have called the city
people by that name. They are clever with the cleverness of the serpent;
and that leads to mischief. Jesus once spoke of the country people as
'babes and sucklings' because of their childlike nature. But the people
of Capernaum He called 'prudent.' God does not like such 'prudence.'
He seeks from us trust in Himself, not trust in our own cleverness."

During the earlier years at Kotgarh and Delhi, when I saw most of
Sundar Singh, his mind often revealed his upbringing as an Indian
villager. Indeed, in his general outlook upon things he was a "villager"
through and through, and he showed a certain contempt for city life.

It was also very striking to notice how little he seemed to care about the great events which were taking place, both in India— owing to the National Movement—and in the world at large. He took no interest in politics: his one supreme concern was religion.

Yet such a confined outlook did not imply any lack of intellectual calibre, for he had a remarkable imagination and was very quick in understanding. He was also amazingly able to describe his deepest thoughts, in a luminous manner, by means of illustrations from his own personal experiences, using these instead of abstract terms. This faculty gave colour to all he saw in ordinary life, and made him a poet at heart.

Thus, his simple, imaginative nature, keenly sensitive to the things of the spirit, fashioned his whole outward character. His deep love of solitude was not due to a negative desire to be alone, but to the mystical sense of an invisible companionship with his Lord. He also had an intense belief in angelic powers surrounding him and keeping him from harm and danger.

Once I heard the story of a moment of extreme peril of imminent death when some Hill-men rescued him from a flooded river in the Himalayas. He believed absolutely that angelic beings bore him up and transported him to the farther shore. He saw them in a vision before he lost consciousness, and when he had come back to life they had disappeared. We are constantly faced, in his own personal records of what happened to him, with narratives of this kind, and I have already written about them.* Such a life of continual wonder and marvel moulded his character and made him what he was—a man who lived more in the unseen world than in the ordinary world of everyday events.

One parallel I have in mind derived from a very early and impressive recollection. At Cambridge, towards the end of last century, I met John G. Paton, the aged missionary from the New Hebrides, and at the same time studied with absorbed interest the story of his early life. He came

---

*   See p. 121.

from a sturdy peasant Covenanting stock at Braehead, in the South of Scotland, and at Tanna he had marvellous experiences of deliverance from imminent peril not unlike those described by Sundar Singh. He had also the same utterly simple and childlike faith in God's protection. I remember well how his face shone as he told us of the miracles that happened to him, and how intensely real they were to him.

With all his love of solitude Sundar Singh was sociable by nature. He was not of the "hermit" type that cannot live with other people, and therefore seeks to dwell apart. Yet even in the midst of a merry company he would suddenly become silent. He would thoroughly enjoy the merriment, and would also take part in it, but his deepest thoughts would wander away elsewhere.

When I knew him only slightly, I used to think of this partial aloofness as due to a shy reserve, for there was always a shyness about him. But I learnt by degrees to understand that he had this habit of silence, which came to him when the mood was on him, and then left him again when the mood changed. Everyone around him was ready to respect it. They took it for granted.

Now and then, while we were at Kotgarh, he would leave us and go out into the silence. He did this so naturally and simply that no one who knew him well took notice of it.

"Where's Sundar?" we would ask sometimes as we came down the hill from Bareri. "Oh, he has gone out to be alone," would be the answer, and after that no further question would be asked.

There was a cave where he would sometimes remain for the sake of solitude, and he would spend there both day and night, until his mood of visionary meditation was over. Then he would come back once more, and we would have the joy of receiving him again into our midst. Such solitude in the forest had its own dangers, especially at night-time, when wild beasts used to come up from the lower jungles. But no wild animal ever hurt the Sadhu.

Closely akin to this love of solitude, I would place his great passion for the supernatural world in which alone he could find peace. This explains, as nothing else can do, many of his actions. It would lead him, for instance, to spend the whole night in prayer, in some solitary place, or on some lonely mountain top. We would see him when he returned, and there would be a serenity about him which was visible to us all. He would speak very little of what he had experienced, but his face itself would tell us what he himself did not reveal.

It was specially at times like these that the habit of trance-like prayer grew upon him. For hours he would remain in ecstasy, taking no food, but with every faculty of the imaginative mind fully alert. Yet when the trance was over it did not seem to have exhausted him, but on the contrary to have been able to bestow upon him new spiritual energy and inner refreshment. It appeared to set him free from his nervous strain, where before it had been bearing hard upon him.

His own devotion to Christ as the living Saviour, with whom he had the closest communion, was increasingly realized as he grew older. So close and personal was this realization that his whole spirit became one with Christ and Christ became one with him.

There is a singularly revealing touch in one of his talks with the Christian ministers of the Gospel in Switzerland. He found it quite difficult, he said, as an Indian Christian, to repeat with fervour the popular hymn, "Nearer, my God, to Thee," because it seemed to picture God in Christ as outside and apart, while his own thought was that of God within, to be realized in the inward heart. Somebody replied to him that the language was only picture-language after all. The Sadhu answered that in India the picture-language which came home to the heart was that which Christ gave to His Church when He said: "I in them and thou in me, that they may be made perfect in one." He also told them how St. John's Gospel, and especially the farewell chapters before the Passion, appealed most of all to his own spirit.*

Without this abiding union with Christ Himself, Sundar Singh's visionary and solitary moods must in the end have led to barrenness and weakness. But instead of this happening, he found a joyous

---

* See *Christ in the Silence*, p. 83.

strength of spirit which enabled him to go through incredible hardships. "During the fourteen years," he relates, "that I have been living
as a Sadhu, there have often been times when stress of hunger, thirst
and persecution might have tempted me to give up this way of life,
had I not just then received the grace of ecstasy. I would not exchange
this gift for the whole world."

He spoke very little concerning these things in public unless he was
challenged to do so. But if at any time it was suggested to him that
they were merely creations of his own fancy, without any reality behind
them, he would assert that they were indeed visions seen by his inner
spirit, rather than incidents external to the mind, but this made them
in no respect less real and effectual in the supernatural sphere. Thus,
when their value was questioned, he always had an answer ready, and
would point to their practical effect upon himself. How could they
give him just the spiritual help he needed, when his own spirit was
failing, unless there was something real about them?

"No, no," he would say, "God uses our human imagination just as
He uses every other faculty of men. The Presence of Christ, which the
eyes of our mind make real to us, is no mere fancy; it is the greatest
reality in the inner world of spirit to-day, without which human life
itself would be impossible of realization in all its fullness."

One other fact became clear to him during the long fast he had
attempted while seeking to follow in Christ's footsteps.* He had often
been troubled with doubts as to whether the extraordinary joy and
peace which accompanied his visions of Christ were due to some hidden
power within his own life, welling up within himself, and not to that
Divine Presence both within and beyond him. He would call in question the source of that inner power, and this often disturbed his prayers.

But while, during this ordeal of the fast, his own bodily powers
both of mind and body decayed, he could feel that the joy and peace
became stronger rather than weaker. This finally convinced him that
these were of divine origin and not self-created and self-imposed.

---

* See Chap IX.

Sundar had also been tempted, he tells us, to wonder what would happen to the spirit when the body and mind were destroyed by death. Would the spirit survive?

When he found, during the fast, that the spirit became even more active than before, while body and mind were both sinking into a comatose state, he became finally assured, that the spirit transcended the mind and had its own independent existence. "The brain," he declared, "is like an organ, and the spirit like an organist who plays upon it. Two or three notes may go wrong, and these may produce no music. But that does not imply the absence of the organist."*

---

* *The Message of Sadhu Sundar Singh,* p. 23.

Chapter XII

His Later Years

THERE was no more beautiful trait in Sadhu Sundar Singh's character than his love for little children. This was noticeable when he came to Europe as well as in the East. It was in keeping with his great humility, and reminded me again and again of the words of Christ:

> "Verily I say unto you, Except ye be converted, and become as little children, ye shall not enter into the kingdom of heaven.
> "Whosoever therefore shall humble himself as this little child, the same is greatest in the kingdom of heaven.
> "And whoso shall receive one such little child in my name receiveth me."

When he was at play with children he would lose all self-consciousness. His shyness also would disappear and he would become a child himself. He had that truly lovable quality of being humble, simple, and at the same time perfectly natural.

A story that illustrates this was told me by Willie Hindle, who was his companion in Lancashire on his first journey to England. He met the Sadhu at Liverpool and took him to be the guest of his sister

111

before he went on to Manchester to stay with Dr. Rendel Harris. In the house were twin boys, who were nearly five years old. After Sundar Singh had arrived, Hindle left him for a few moments in order to look after the necessary arrangements for his comfort. On coming down a little later, he found the Sadhu down on his hands and knees, with the twins climbing over him, to their huge delight. All the painful nervousness of this, his first visit in a strange country, had vanished in the presence of these two young children.

He had to leave very early the next morning with Willie Hindle, his friend. At the breakfast table, later, one of the twins said to his mother: "Mummy, where has Jesus gone to?"

"Hush, darling," said the mother, "that wasn't Jesus; that was Sadhu Sundar Singh."

"No, Mummy," said the little one, "*I* know who he was. That *was* Jesus! And I know where he's gone to. He's gone to heaven and taken Uncle Willie with him!"

This story might be repeated in various ways from other incidents which happened during his visits to the West. For often, when a door was opened, or when he went into a room, someone or other would be struck by his appearance, which seemed to bring with it the presence of Christ, his Lord. The Master was thus made visible through the disciple, and little children in their innocence of heart were the first to notice it. So they ran to his arms without any fear.

Of all the joys that his visits to the West brought him, there was none, perhaps, that gave him greater happiness than this instinctive love which the children everywhere seemed ready to give him. While it humbled him to be thus mistaken for his Lord and Master, it gave him a deep inner joy to know for certain that he was able in this manner to bring Christ's presence with him and to make it felt by others.   ,

Though the Sadhu had his silent moods, wherein he seemed to be brooding over some distant prospect, and these were often mingled with sadness, there were other times when he was absurdly and intensely human, full of fun and happy laughter. He was fortunate in thus being able to let his mind entirely relax. A bubbling spring of whimsical humour seemed to be on the point of overflowing. It burst forth on the most unlikely subjects. When he was in the hospital with one of his eyes completely blinded by an ulcer, which caused him exquisite pain, he said to a friend who was deeply sympathizing with him: "At least I can say now that my eye is single"—referring to the fact that he had only one eye left to see with.

On another occasion, when he was in the lift of the Eiffel Tower, in Paris, and the party had reached the third floor and were looking down at the earth below: "Now," he said, "we can all of us say with St. Paul that we have been caught up to the third heaven."

At other times, when impatience got the better of him, he could be caustic as well as absurd. "Sadhu," asked a lady in Switzerland, "do you ever find snakes in the railway trains in India?" "No," he replied, quickly raising his head, "they don't travel there— not even in the first or second class!" And then he broke out into a peal of happy laughter in which everyone joined, including the lady herself.

His humour would sometimes take the form of action, especially with those who were eager to make too much of him and treat him as a kind of superior being. He disliked this intensely, and if ever he sensed it in the atmosphere around him he might suddenly leave the room and thus bring things down to a more human level. He could not "suffer fools gladly."

Yet he deeply regretted the hastiness of his temper, which showed itself when he was tired. He would do his utmost to overcome it at the time and would spend long hours of silence afterwards seeking to regain full self-control. Thoughtless questions used to vex him most of all. "That question," he would answer, "is not useful."

He grew very weary during long interpretations of his sentences by translators and would pull them by their coat-tails and ask them to be short. He felt that these long translations made the audience restless, and a restless audience troubled him greatly. On the continent of Europe this was evidently one of the things which caused him most exhaustion, and at the end of his visit in 1922 he was worn out. Few realized the strain which his sensitive mind, accustomed to the ways of village India, endured while he was longing and praying that his message concerning Christ, his Master, should sink deeply into men's hearts and bear fruit in their lives.

During his tour in the United States he happened to see outside the hall where he was speaking his own name posted, and underneath it the title, "Apostle of India." He mentions this with horror and adds the words in Urdu: "When I saw it, I went into a cold sweat." The absurdity of such a grandiloquent title filled him with shame. Yet he could not always prevent it.

Even in his illustrations of sacred subjects he sometimes allowed his keen enjoyment of an absurd analogy to have full play. "When we see a crane," he writes, "standing motionless on the side of a tank, we may suppose from his attitude that he is musing on the glory of God, or the excellent quality of the water. But no such thing! He stands there motionless for hours; but the moment he catches sight of a frog or a small fish, he springs upon it and gulps it down. Just such is the attitude of many with regard to prayer. Seated by the shore of the boundless ocean of God's love, they are wrapped up in the one thought of acquiring some specially required object!"

No one without a strong sense of humour could have drawn a picture parable like this!

While he remained simple and childlike to the end, trusting to instinctive judgments rather than to logical processes of reasoning, his mind showed at times a creative power of thought of a very high order. Some of his sentences cling to the imagination once they have been heard, and will not leave it.

He pictures Christ as saying to the disciple: "When a man turns towards Me in true repentance, I cleanse the temple of his heart with the whips of love and make it a heavenly abode for the King of kings."

Again he describes Christ as saying: "With My finger I wrote upon the ground the sinful state of each of those who brought the sinful woman to Me for condemnation.... With My finger, too, I point out in secret to My servants their wounds of sin; and when they repent, with a touch of the same finger I heal them."

Once more he gives these words to the lips of Christ: "The womb of Mary, where in a fleshly form I had My abode for a few months, was not a place so blessed as the heart of the believer, in which for all time I have My home and make it a heaven."*

There is a greatness of conception in such sentences as these which lifts them far above the commonplace. There is the same note of greatness in many of his parables and illustrations. Sometimes they fail to impress, but more often they remain in the mind and can be thought over again and again.

After his visits to Europe and America, when English had become familiar to him, he was wont to read English books far more widely than before. When I looked through the small library that he had left behind at Sabathu, it became clear at once from those he had selected that modem science had begun to have a great attraction for him. He had underlined in pencil every book he read, and it was quite a revelation to me to find out how widely he had studied and what were his special interests. Books on psychology and mysticism were heavily marked. Volumes such as William James's *Varieties of Religious Experience*, Mother Julian's *Revelations of Divine Love*, Raymond Lull, Boehme, Swedenborg and others had been studied with deep attention.

One large illustrated book, called *Outline of Science*, was carefully pencilled throughout. A press notice had been pasted on the fly-leaf, with underlining, which showed why he had been eager to pursue this subject and how closely it had affected his mind.

"Every thoughtful person," it runs, "deplores the present prevalence of sensational superstitions, but it is becoming clear that such superstitions can only be combated by showing that alleged *supernatural marvels can for the most part be explained, as natural in accordance with psychological law.*

* These quotations are from *At the Master's Feet*, published by Fleming H. Revell Co.

"It is evident, however, that much religious experience, which has been regarded as beyond human interpretation, will be shown, by the same means, to be in accordance with the natural laws of mind."

In this significant quotation I have represented the Sadhu's under-linings by italics. His evident agreement with the drift of the passage seems to indicate an advance in his own mind with regard to the miraculous stories which he had brought forward and allowed to be published in earlier years. In proportion to his increasing knowledge of scientific thought, he appeared to have sought more and more to interpret what he had seen during spiritual visions and ecstasies according to the natural laws of mind. He had a great reverence for the intellect of man and did not dispute its valid judgments. At the same time he fully believed that there were laws of the spiritual world which had yet to be explored.

There was one small book which showed the heaviest marking of all. It was called *A Gentleman in Prison.** This volume gives a remarkable account of the last days of a Japanese prisoner, named Ishii, who was converted to Christianity in a very marvellous manner within the prison walls. The intense joy of his new Christian experience, after his conversion, seemed to have impressed itself most of all on Sundar Singh's imagination. So heavily is this one volume marked in pencil that there are marginal lines which cover whole chapters. To go through the book with all its markings reveals much in the character of the Sadhu himself. Since his own copy of the book was only published in 1927, it must have been among the last that he added to his library, and the eager enthusiasm with which he read it is apparent.

One of the marked passages, written just before Ishii's execution, reads as follows:

"I have entered the City of God, where the soul cannot perish! *My daily joy is indescribable!*

---

* Translated by the late Caroline Macdonald. Published by the Student Christian Movement Press, London.

> To-day I have entered the City of God!
> My name is defiled,
> My body dies in prison,
> But my soul, purified,
> To-day returns to the City of God!"

Even more deeply lined still is a chapter called "The Gifts of the Prison House," where Ishii places on record the "three divine favours" which he had received from God when he became a Christian.

"I want to tell you," he writes from prison, "what divine favours were given to me after I became a believer in Christ.

"First, I received the imperishable and eternal salvation of that most important part of man, his soul. As it is written, 'Him that cometh unto me, I will in no wise cast out.'

SCRIPTURE TESTIMONY
Jesus will never send away those who come to Him
JOHN 6:37
Father forgive them, for they know not what they do
LUKE 23:34 · ACTS 7:60

"It was only after I had got into prison that I came to believe that man really has a soul, and I shall tell you how I came to see this. In the prison yard, chrysanthemums have been planted to please the eyes of the inmates. When the season comes they bear beautiful flowers, but in the winter they are nipped by the frost and wither. Our outer eye tells us that the flowers are dead, but this is not the real truth. When the season returns the buds sprout once more and the beautiful flowers bloom again. And so I cannot but believe that if God in His mercy does not allow even the flowers to die, there surely is a soul in man which He intends shall live for ever.

"I shall now speak of a second favour which I have received from God. When I was free I travelled about, West and East, out in the world, and saw and heard many things, and had varied experiences. Today I am sitting in my prison cell with no liberty to come and go, and yet I am far more contented than in the days of my freedom. In prison, with only poor coarse food to eat, I am more thankful than I ever was out in the world when I could get whatever food I wanted. In this prison cell, only nine feet by six feet in size, I am happier than if I was living in the largest house I ever saw in the outer world. Whatever agony is in my heart I can now overcome. No matter what discomforts I endure there is only gladness in my heart. The joy of each day is very great. These things are all due to the grace and divine favour of Jesus Christ.

"I wish to speak now of the greatest favour of all—the power of Christ, which cannot be measured by any of our standards. I have been more than twenty years in prison since I was nineteen years of age, and during that time I have known what it meant to endure suffering, although I have had some pleasant times as well. I have passed through all sorts of experiences, and have been urged often to repent of my sins. In spite of this, however, I did not repent, but on the contrary became more and more hardened. And then by the power of that one word of Christ's, 'Father, forgive them, for they know not what they do,' my unspeakably hardened heart was changed, and I repented of all my crimes. Such power is not in man."

Every sentence of this long passage is heavily marked with pencil, and the book itself is almost worn out by constant use. The Sadhu must have returned to it many times in the last year of his life for comfort and inspiration. In a singular manner it seemed to have recalled to him his own deep joy in Christ which followed his conversion.

As I went through all his books, one by one, with his handwriting here and there in the margin, and his pencil marks everywhere scattered over the pages, it was a very moving experience. It seemed as if a veil had been removed and the Sadhu had laid bare his own soul. There was the same essentially simple, humble and childlike mind which I had known in the past. But all his intellectual powers had surprisingly matured. He had set himself to understand what was for him another hemisphere of human thought, strangely unlike his own. Scientific knowledge seemed to have left him on the whole sorely bewildered, but he had held fast to the one fundamental principle underlying all his actions, namely, his heart devotion to Christ. With him as he gazed into this new world, "Christ was the beginning and the end was Christ."

There was one problem in my own mind concerning these closing years which I had not been able to solve. Therefore, I asked many of his closest friends about it. When I had met him last, in 1926, there had been a deep sadness in his face which troubled me a great deal. But I had not been able to discover whether it had become a constant feature with him or had only been a passing cloud. Those whom I approached had noticed this sadness also, but I was relieved to find how everyone felt that it had not become habitual with him. They spoke of his inner joy in Christ always continuing, as an abiding treasure, in spite of his outward pain.

The Bishop of Lahore, Dr. Bame, had lived for many years close to Sabathu, at Sanawar. Both he and his wife had known the Sadhu intimately over a long series of years. His personal knowledge made him quite clear on that point.

"I detected," he wrote to me, "no difference from the time when I first knew him up to the April, 1929, when I saw him last, just before he set out on his last journey. He came and said good-bye to me and told me he hoped to be back in the autumn. Sundar used to stay with us. He always joined in ordinary meals. When he was ill and in great pain from his eye, my wife used to say sometimes at dinner: 'Sadhuji, you look very tired: a glass of wine will do you good? His usual answer was: 'If you think so, I will certainly take it: all things are good? Surely this was always more or less his normal attitude. His house at Sabathu (which he shared with the two Catechists from the Leper Asylum) had one nicely furnished room which contained the Sadhu's books and some photographs.

"Bishop Durrant and I went over to see him there once. He gave us a meal nicely served, but he did not eat anything on that occasion himself. I rather gathered that he had had it specially prepared for us: that it was not the normal meal of the house, even though it was very simple. His dress remained more or less the same, though he sometimes wore a saffron garment more in the nature of a cassock. It was in 1927 or 1928, I think, that we saw a good deal of him. He stayed in our house and I took him to the ophthalmic specialist in Kasauli. During that time he often abstracted himself for hours on end to the spirit world, sitting in his room, and came back much refreshed.

"Incidentally the room he occupied was supposed to be haunted. Some people who slept there used to speak of a presence of which they had been aware if they were psychical. Since the Sadhu used that room and 'left' the world, no one has ever referred to the presence again. Perhaps he got into touch with some wandering spirit and satisfied him? Who knows?

"I should not have described Sundar's face then as sad: it was wistful. The 'deep sadness' you refer to was not in evidence. He was suffering and that had its effect. During that time he nearly always spoke about our Lord. Whatever he started on he came back to Him. Christ filled his life. 'To me, to live is Christ,' was obviously the motto of his life. I have never met anybody in my life of whom this was more literally and absolutely true."

This letter carries forward the record of the Sadhu's life right up to its close, for the Bishop saw him just before he left Sabathu for his last journey into Tibet.

Canon Chandu Lal, of Simla, went over the same ground with me which the Bishop had covered in his letter. He agreed with me that a deep sadness had grown upon the Sadhu in his later years, which was chiefly due to his continual ill-health; but he told me also of the joy in Christ which remained radiant with him and made him able to rise above his physical weakness. Sundar Singh, he said, had an intense longing for death which seemed to become stronger and stronger. All through those painful years of suffering his deep humility and penitence were very touching to witness. .For him to live was Christ.

One other friend, the Rev. T. E. Riddle, gave me valuable detailed information.

"I saw the Sadhu," he wrote to me, "from time to time, and stayed with him while I was translating his books. He persistently spoke to me of the weakness of his Jungs and his frequent heart-attacks, whereas the root of all his trouble seems to have been gastric. After 1924 a considerable degree of heart discomfort followed almost all his public meetings. On several occasions the heart-attacks were

SCRIPTURE TESTIMONY
True disciples love Jesus more than even their own lives
MATTHEW 8:18-22 · MATTHEW 16:21-28 · LUKE 9:57-62 · LUKE 14:25-35
The fulness of God's joy comes through obedience
JOHN 15:11 · GALATIANS 5:22 · PHILIPPIANS 4:4 · HEBREWS 12:2

so severe as to leave him unconscious for hours at a time. On his attempt to go to Tibet in 1927, a very severe hemorrhage from the stomach made his Tibetan fellow travellers take him back to the railway. During his last years his letters were full of references to his poor health, and I have seen him dazed with the pain of an attack that was mild compared with others.

"For him the indwelling of Christ was no mere intellectual conception. It was a reality to which his whole experience gave increasing witness. He put Christ in the centre of all his thinking, and 'self' receded more and more out of the picture. The sense of harmony between his surrendered life and the Indwelling Lord was an unending source of peace and joy to him. In hours of specially intense spiritual stress, when suffering deprivation for Christ's sake, the joy that came to him used to wipe away all the pain. He would explain that it was not joy in suffering, but that the pain itself was transmuted into joy.

"There was no pride in him. He always marvelled that the Lord had chosen him for world fame. He seldom mentioned his 'visions.' There was nothing abnormal about him. He delighted in human joy and loved a joke, but he would leave the merriest party to go to his tryst with his Lord. He was a man who saw the glory of God in the face of Jesus Christ."

Whenever I look back on his whole life and remember what he had to go through, one feature appears to me to be outstanding. His faith and courage, inspired by a childlike confidence in God's guidance, enabled him to face dangers and endure hardships from which the bravest would have recoiled. Only one whose life was passed in the supernatural world of prayer, inspired by a love of Christ stronger than any earthly love, could have taken such terrible risks alone, with absolutely no other resource except the divine aid.

It was not with him as it is with a traveller who has taken every possible precaution beforehand and is thus prepared to run great risks. Rather he went alone, time after time, as a Sadhu, carrying nothing with him. What hunger and nakedness, what pain and illness of body, what insult and humiliation of spirit he suffered during his wanderings, only those can understand who have tried this life year after year. The wonder is, not that he appears now to have succumbed, but that this fate had not overtaken him many years ago.

Chapter XIII

Is He Dead?

A SHORT notice in *The Times* of London, which appeared in other newspapers all over the world on April 28th, 1933, announced as follows:

"The probate of Sadhu Sundar Singh's Will has been granted in India as a consequence of the official presumption of his death by the Government of India on the ground that there has been no news of him since 1929, when he visited Tibet."

Is Sadhu Sundar Singh really dead?

When I was in India in 1933, I found out from every side that the question was still being debated. Two views were held almost equally strongly by his different friends.

On the one side, it was firmly believed that he had silently retired into the fastnesses of the Himalayas in order to lead a solitary life of prayer away from the world. Thus the Bishop of Lahore wrote to me: "I wonder, is he dead? Quite a number of people believe he is still living. Charles Ibrahim, who is our Indian priest at Sanawar, absolutely refuses to believe that the Sadhu is not alive, and he tells me many share his view."

On the other side, many who knew him best were convinced, owing to the long period of silence which has now elapsed since April, 1929, that he is already dead.

"We should have heard something of him," they said to me, "if he had been still alive. For he promised to come back in the autumn."

A letter written by Mr. Watson, Superintendent of the Leper Asylum of Sabathu, dated September 3rd, 1929, gave at the time, in a concise manner, the main facts concerning his last journey into Tibet. Many rumours have been current since then, and more than once he has been reported to be alive; but not one of these reports, on careful inquiry being made, can be proved to have any truth at the back of it. The silence remains unbroken.

Mr. Watson described how Sundar Singh called in at the Leper Asylum to bid him farewell on April 13th, just before he was starting off on his journey to Tibet. In a previous year he had left Sabathu with the same end in view, and just at the same time of year, in the month of April, when the mountain passes are open. But after going on foot along the broad road which is called the "Pilgrim Line," for a distance of forty miles from Rishikesh, he was taken suddenly ill with severe hemorrhage from the stomach, and was brought back to the railhead by some of his Tibetan fellow travellers, who saw him through in safety to the train. From there he was able to travel back to Sabathu, where he slowly recovered his health.

In the same manner, in April, 1929—Mr. Watson relates—he had left his home at Sabathu in order to join the Tibetan traders, with whom he had corresponded beforehand about his journey. He had intended to accompany them across the snow mountains into Tibet. They were to travel for some distance along the well-trodden pilgrim route, which leads to the sacred Hindu shrine at Badrinath. The Tibetan caravan would then branch off from this road before reaching Badrinath itself; for the mountain track into Tibet would go more to the east through the Niti Pass. The Sadhu had promised Mr. Watson that, if God willed, he hoped to return by the same route and reach Sabathu about the end of June. Since he would be entirely out of reach of the post, he asked Mr. Watson to receive his correspondence and to reply to any letters that needed an immediate answer. In case of illness, the Sadhu had promised to send messengers, if possible, to Sabathu. Meanwhile, he left instructions about his will, which his two executors were to carry out if he did not return.

Mr. Watson's letter to me from Sabathu, dated November 20th, 1933, gives some further details, both about the last years of the Sadhu's life and also concerning those closing days before he started on the journey from which he never returned.

"During the years," Mr. Watson writes, "in which I knew the Sadhu, he did not go out on many preaching tours, and then only for briefer periods than in the early days of his work. At home he used to spend a good many hours at his correspondence and literary work. His letters must have been many; for after he left us, letters came to him from all over the world. He had asked me to receive his correspondence when he left for the tour to Tibet. Before he left, he more than once spoke to me as if he felt he might never return alive. But he was quite prepared, he told me, for whatever was God's will. He seemed to have the premonition that he had not long to live; but he said he did not fear death.

"I shook hands with him at the gateway to our house, and was probably the last European to do so before he disappeared. Sannu Lal, our Indian preacher for the leper work, went with him a part of the way to Kalka station, where he intended to take the train for Rishikesh, and thence on foot through Garhwal along the banks of the Ganges towards Badrinath, and thence over the Niti Pass into Tibet itself. You will know how his friend and executor, Rev. T. E. Riddle of Kharar, and Dr. Taylor of Roorkee, went all the way, later on, to try and trace him. I also spoke to the Superintendent of Police when he was here on tour and also when I saw him in Simla. No one, after he left Kalka, seems to have noticed him, even though he would Be wearing his long saffron robe and dark glare glasses. His last letter to me was written two days before he left, on April 18th, 1929. It was in answer to a query I had received from Calcutta. He wrote:

"'Thank you for your note of yesterday. Yes, please answer the query that I shall be going on a long evangelistic tour on Thursday, 18th inst., and hope to visit, God willing, Calcutta next winter. I have written to Brother Irvine that I am leaving my correspondence in your charge, and also to our friend Mr. Riddle. I know that he will be very glad that you would kindly help him to arrange things here, in case something happens to me on this difficult tour. Acts 20:24. I will come and see you before I leave for Tibet. I know that you will be helping me by your prayers, for which I thank you heartily.

"'With love in the Lord, yours in Him,

"'SUNDAR SINGH.'

"During the summer of 1925 he had gone on a week-end tour north of Sabathu into the villages with a missionary friend, and during that time he got some eye trouble, which did not seem to get cured. He didn't consider at first that it was serious. Nevertheless, this resulted in the sight of one eye being almost lost; and afterwards he always wore dark glasses. Months after, he had expert advice, but even an operation did not restore the lost vision in that one eye. The other was all right.

"Throughout the four years I knew him at Sabathu, he did not leave his rooms much, and it was only once that I persuaded him to speak at a public meeting for Hindus and Mohammedans and all comers. He said the people here knew him and could visit him for talks whenever they desired.... He felt that his articles for magazines in different countries and his books would reach a larger audience, and so he spent his time at that work.

"Personally, I feel that in the last few years he did not have sufficient physical exercise.... I suggested to him, before he started, that for a few weeks he should take more strenuous exercise than just a gentle walk round the hill here for a mile but he laughed and said he would be ready for the journey."

When the time had passed by, and no news came through at all, Mr. Riddle, of the New Zealand Presbyterian Mission, who was one of the two executors, determined to go out in company with Dr. Taylor of Roorkee in search of the Sadhu, along the way he expected to travel. They spent nearly a month in hard travelling to within four miles of Tibet, reaching an altitude of 18,000 feet, and often, finding themselves in serious danger. But they could not find any trace of the Sadhu at all. Strangely enough, no one seemed to have heard of him along that route. Government officials had also searched through the pilgrim registers at the different halting-places, but no record had been found there, and the whole search had to be abandoned.

The hemorrhage, which had occurred on his previous journey, is referred to by different friends who saw him on that occasion after his return. The Sadhu himself, who had suffered from the same illness before, firmly believed that it was a symptom of tuberculosis. But those who knew him best have assured me that his fear was groundless, and that the hemorrhage came from the stomach. Yet it was no less serious on that account. His whole physical condition, in those later years of his life, was such that no journey at all into the high altitudes of Tibet ought ever to have been undertaken. It was courting death to make such a march in feeble health. But no power on earth could persuade the Sadhu to give up the lifelong struggle which he felt to be divinely appointed. Many had tried to dissuade him, but none had succeeded.

The story of the search-party has been graphically told by Mr. Riddle in a magazine which was widely quoted in the Indian papers. I was unable to meet Mr. Riddle personally, but he has most kindly given me every help and placed his own notes at my disposal. Before starting in April, 1929, the Sadhu sent a letter to him stating that he expected either himself to be back at Landour, or to send word there, sometime early in July. But he never came.

Mr. Riddle relates how the Sadhu had written to him in the same terms as he had written to Mr. Watson, but he had added some further details. He had said that he intended to go in company with a Tibetan trader up the "Pilgrim Line" to a place near Badrinath, where the road into Tibet turns off and follows the course of the Dauli River till the

Niti Pass is reached. He was to visit some Christian families, who were living towards the east of Lake Manasarowar.

The account given by Mr. Riddle shows clearly how almost impossible the mountain track into Tibet would have been for a sick man with his eyesight seriously damaged to travel over, when once the "Pilgrim Line" had been left behind. Bad slips were encountered from the very beginning of the journey. The pack-mule had to be unloaded again and again in order to cross the gaps in the road. One of the Hill-men who accompanied them went suddenly down with fever. When at last they were able to move forward, they found that the bridges ahead were all unsafe, and some had been swept away.

"Across a span," he writes, "of fifty feet, with a cataract roaring below, three pine logs had been thrown, but it was a long span, and the logs were neither supported below nor were their ends fixed. There was about a foot between each log, and they rolled under our feet and bobbed up and down deliriously as, with set teeth, we picked our steps across. One of the Hill-men could not face it with a load but crawled over on his hands and knees.

"Next day we managed to hire two Bhotia ponies and set out on the eight miles' climb to the top of the Hoti Pass on the border of Tibet. Beyond that we could not go, as we had given our promise to the Deputy Commissioner not to cross over. We started at daylight, and soon reached a road-slip on a wet and slippery hill where there was only a goat track across. We climbed steadily between two walls of rugged mountains for four miles. There we came across three men cowering over a fire. Their teeth were chattering with cold and they were trembling violently. They said they were perished with cold as they had been out in the rain and snow all night."

The Bhotias had warned them about the fearful blizzard which blew through the pass every day at midday and warned them not to remain at the head of the pass during that interval. The altitude of 18,000 feet was terribly trying, and the glare of the dazzling snow had given them violent headaches which might have led on to snow-blindness. Clouds covered the plateau of Tibet which lay below them. So, they reluctantly returned without having seen the Forbidden Land. A Tibetan caravan passed them as it hurried along in order to get down from the pass before the icy wind began at midday. As they accompanied it for a short distance, the leader told them how, on the last occasion of crossing, the caravan had lost six men in the cold of the pass before safety was reached.

On their return journey, they encountered once more bridges which were down and slips in the road where it had broken away. They found one of the bridges, which they had crossed only a few days before, now completely washed away by a sudden spate which had brought great blocks of mountain rock rolling downwards from the heights. They were obliged to make a wide detour, till they reached a valley where the shepherds had become cut off from their supplies by another bridge which had been destroyed by the swollen river.

The rest of the description I must give in Mr. Riddle's own words:

"The shepherds told us," he writes, "that there was a difficult, but possible, track round. So we crossed over to try it. The Dauli River runs through an immense 'fault,' with sheer precipices on either side, where each ridge in turn has been shorn in two by some ancient upheaval. As a road, it did not look promising, but it appeared to be the only way.

"The first climb was up 2,000 feet of sheer cliff, with little to hang on to and a long way to drop. After we had crawled up and then round the point, we crossed a stream, and then climbed over the back of another hill and had a thousand feet straight down, over rock faces, before we could get round the foot of the next cliff. Then we had to face another 2,000 foot hill, with an eighteen-inch ledge, which led round three bluffs. Finally we had to go back up two miles of mountain track before we could get down the cliffs of a cross stream and when we got there, tired and hungry and in the dusk, we found that the bridge there had gone too.

"We slept under a cliff with fourteen others who, like ourselves, were held up. Next morning we were out at daylight. On the stones in front a pine log was lying. It was thirty-five feet long. Some previous flood had stripped it of its branches and left it stranded at this very crossing. We put its end in a gap between two rocks on the edge of the water, and with the help of the men, rammed it over against the far bank. Then we ran a life-line over it, and the whole party were soon across."

Mr. Riddle ends his remarkable journal by summing up the negative report which he brought back. No trace of the Sadhu had been found along the mountain track into Tibet. It therefore appeared almost certain that he did not pass that way. Furthermore, he failed to reach some Christians whom he had hoped to visit in the interior. If he had passed that way he would surely have gone to see them. On the "Pilgrim Line" itself there was also no trace of him; but that was hardly to be expected, because fifty to sixty thousand pilgrims crowd that part of the road every year during April and May.

Mr. Riddle concludes as follows: "Then what happened? Did death meet him on the way? His health was not good and cholera was bad on the 'Pilgrim Line' in May and June. Perhaps he went out that way and left no trace; for there, bodies are at once taken up, and without identification cast into the waters of the Ganges in the hope that Ganga Mai (Mother Ganges) will bear them away to eternal bliss. We do not know. Perhaps we shall never know. But we are making further inquiries through the British Agent in Western Tibet, in order to see if the Sadhu ever reached his objective there."

This striking narrative provides us with detailed information concerning the difficulties of this road by way of the Niti Pass into Tibet. Sundar Singh had already attempted it, on previous occasions, for it was the only alternative route to the Hindustan-Tibet Road which runs past Kotgarh. His object in starting his journey by way of the "Pilgrim Line" was evidently to get into touch with the Hindu pilgrims on their march to Badrinath. Since Tibetan caravans went along this road, he would have the further advantage of travelling in their company. Probably he intended to use a mule or Bhotia pony for this journey, since walking up and down the steep mountain tracks would have been out of the question with the heart trouble from which he suffered. Starting before the full melting of the snows, he would not meet with the difficulties of bridges washed away, which Mr. Riddle and Dr. Taylor encountered. Nevertheless, as can be easily realized from their narrative, this track by way of the Niti Pass is difficult in the extreme.

It is indeed strange that the Sadhu was ever allowed to attempt such a journey in his enfeebled health, with both heart and stomach weakness and one of his eyes blinded. The truth was, as I have already related, that in all these personal matters, he possessed an iron determination which none even of his dearest friends could shake, however dangerous the course might seem that he was pursuing. Whenever he believed that he was called upon, under Divine guidance, to undertake anything, he endeavoured to perform it, in spite of any illness that might result from it to himself.

Chapter XIV

The Answer

THE question remains to be answered, since no positive proof of his death has ever been given—"Is it possible that the Sadhu may be still living in the vast solitudes of the Himalaya Mountains?"

Among his closest friends in India it was deeply touching to me to find how that expectation of seeing him again lingered on and on, in spite of the number of years that have now passed since he set out to go into Tibet.

There were three distinct forms which the argument for his survival took. It will be well to consider them apart.

The first argument was put to me by an old pupil of my own in Delhi, who was quite positive that die Sadhu was alive.

"Sadhuji and I," he said to me, "had very many talks together about this very thing. He expressed a great desire not only to go into Tibet to preach the Gospel, but also to spend the last days of his life in solitary prayer and meditation. He told me a great deal concerning the hermits he had met in the recesses of the Himalayas, and explained to me how he longed to spend all his time in silence. Since his exhausting journeys all over the world, he had felt more and more the call to this greater life of silent prayer from some mountain top, where all the world could be brought into the mind's view and be remembered before the Throne of God. His very eagerness to get away each year into Tibet, in spite of his failing health, had revealed his longing for a retreat where he might be alone with God in the silence, and thus fulfil a deeper ministry than any round of desultory daily tasks could accomplish."

The second argument came from some of the Sadhu's friends who had watched anxiously the later years of his life at close quarters, and had noticed the distress which had come to him from those who had doubted his veracity, and had written books and articles about him impugning his good faith. While his courage in facing physical dangers was incredibly great, he was prone to brood on the things that wounded his inner spirit. When the blow came to him from that side, he shrank back like a stricken thing, and the iron of it entered his soul.

As one who had known him intimately, I could easily appreciate the force of the argument, when one after another of his friends told me how much he had longed in later years to be far away from the strife of tongues and the noise of controversy, where he might be silently at peace with his Master. This extreme sensitiveness was a weakness, it is true, but it was a human frailty which made him nearer to ourselves just where we thought he might have been strongest.

"What could be more natural," his friends said to me, "than for the Sadhu, when he was weary and sick, in body and soul alike, to go silently apart in order to fulfil at last his own heart's deepest desire. He may not have started from Sabathu with that object clearly before him, but the way may have been opened out to him as he went on. He was a Sadhu, who passed to and fro as the Spirit moved him, and no one could be quite certain what might be the next step he would take."

A touching record came into my hands while I was thinking over this very question, which shows how very deeply this controversy concerning his veracity had affected his inner life. In a personal letter to Mrs. Parker, which she has allowed me to quote, he tells in Urdu a remarkable dream.

"I was sitting," he writes, "in a valley, and saw the mists rising until they formed a cloud so thick that the sky was blotted out by it. Then I saw very heavy rain descend and the sky became clear again and even brighter than before. After a short time an elder came to me and said: 'I will show you the meaning of what you have seen: this valley is the world, and the mists are the evil and hostile thoughts which rise up against the Lord's servants and form a cloud blotting out the Lord Himself and the sky. But do not be downcast, because just as the mists that rise from the earth descend in fruitful rain, so these evil and hostile thoughts will fall to the ground, and the servants of the Lord will see the sky far, far brighter than before.'

"After he had said this my eyes were opened, and immediately I wrote down what I had seen. And now, my dearest mother, if men speak ill of me, do not be troubled, but rejoice."

We are told by those who have studied the laws of the mind that dreams often denote that which is very deeply hidden in the subconscious part of our being. Sundar Singh brooded far too much over the attacks which had been made upon him. He tried hard inwardly to conquer this weakness, but the strain to his hypersensitive nature was very great indeed.

The third argument which was put before me in favour of his being still living and leading a solitary life of retirement, ran in some such way as this: There are certain instincts which are very deep-rooted in India among religious people, and one of them is the intense desire for retirement into solitude which comes upon men and women as youth is left behind and old age advances.

The Sadhu, though still comparatively young in years, had grown old very rapidly in his inner nature after his exhausting journeys both in Tibet and in the West. The life which he had been leading before he went to Europe had made solitude a necessity for him, and there had also grown up in him a deep longing for the remoteness of the high mountains, where he might be alone with the Divine Source of all created life. This had become like a home-sickness to him.

Far more deeply than in the West, such a longing for retirement is regarded in India as both natural in itself and also in keeping with the deep needs of man's inner spirit. With these innate instincts so strong in him from childhood, there would be nothing strange if the Sadhu, by some sudden act of his own, had cut himself off from his fellow-men. Even though he might have set out on his journey to Tibet with the full intention of returning, this overwhelming impulse urging him to solitude might have come over him with such force that he could not refuse to carry it out to the end.

While I have wandered up and down India and visited the pilgrims' centres, I have constantly seen at retired spots, such as Brindaban, Hardwar, and elsewhere, men and women who have entirely left their own domestic circles in order to end their lives in meditation and prayer without any interruption from the outer world. I have been often told also that in the remote mountains of India there are others who follow a similar course. When I spoke with one such devotee at Brindaban, he told me that for nearly twenty years he had been thus living the life of solitude on the banks of the River Jumna, and that all thought of returning to active life had long ago been abandoned.

In all that I have written down above, my aim has been to give force to the arguments which have been brought forward to me by those who are still certain that the Sadhu is living in retirement. Each of them appears to me to possess some force, and it would be impossible to rule them out altogether in the light of the long silence that has been unbroken since the Sadhu left Sabathu in April, 1929. But while these considerations gain for a moment an air of credibility when thus stated, their likelihood becomes less when further tests are applied.

For all three arguments are clearly based on the supposition that Sundar Singh definitely changed his mind at some point on his journey into Tibet. Yet all the facts at our disposal appear to go directly against this.

The simplest fact of all is surely his own declared intention to return after a few months' absence, if God spared his life. He had gone into

Tibet many times before at the same season of the year, and had returned later, before the hard frosts began which would make a return journey impossible. He had tried to accomplish this same journey into Tibet as late as the year 1927, and had only failed through serious illness on the way. He was taking the same route in 1929. Furthermore, he had decided, by going through the Niti valley, to visit a small group of isolated Christians who badly needed his aid. He would not be likely to omit such a positive duty to his Christian converts if he had been able to reach them on his march.

In addition to all these things, the Sadhu had left a precise message with Mr. Watson concerning his correspondence, and he had promised to send a messenger if he was taken ill on the road. He had also written a letter to Mrs. Parker saying that he would return at the end of the summer. No one was held by the Sadhu in greater reverence and affection than Mrs. Parker, whom he always called his "mother." Lately I have been looking through bundles of letters from him, which Mrs. Parker had carefully kept. In every one of them his deep love for her is manifest, and also his concern to save her from the slightest anxiety on his account. He had written to her on previous occasions before starting for Tibet, and each time he had definitely faced the prospect of death on such a journey. More than once in later years, before starting out, he had quoted the passage from the Acts of the Apostles, where St. Paul bade farewell to the elders of the Church at Ephesus. The passage may be quoted in full at this place, since it reveals to us the Sadhu's own mind.

> "Behold, I go bound in the spirit into Jerusalem, not knowing the things that shall befall me there:
>
> "Save that the Holy Ghost witnesseth in every city, saying that bonds and afflictions abide me.
>
> "But none of these things move me, neither count I my life dear unto myself, so that I might finish my course with joy, and the ministry, which I have received of the Lord Jesus, to testify the gospel of the grace of God.

"And now, behold, I know that ye all, among whom I have
gone preaching the kingdom of God, shall see my face no
more."*

These elaborate preparations appear to me to be much too carefully planned, after earnest prayer and seeking divine guidance, for
any cancellation merely owing to a different mood coming over him,
which he had not sufficient inward strength to resist. He was not so
easily swayed as that.

No! The root of the difficulty lies further back. The problem surely
is this, that he should have decided, when his general health was so
bad and his heart was so weak, to take this impossible journey at all.
An answer has first to be given here before other questions are asked.

We have already seen how desperately he tried to struggle on and
accomplish the journey in 1927, until hemorrhage drove him back.
While he appeared to be a little stronger in the spring of 1928, and
took active part in the Bareilly Christian Convention, he was in very
weak health all the rest of the year, and those who met him at Kotgarh
in the autumn were alarmed by his increasing weakness.

Chand Mal, the son of Professor Khub Ram, was staying during
that autumn with his father near to Kotgarh. They both used to meet
Sundar Singh, who was living a retired life at the house of Padre Philip.
Both Chand Mal and his father have told me how very weak the
Sadhu was. He could not venture to climb any steep ascent because
of heart trouble. Indeed, he had to pause and take breath after walking a short distance. How could he think of undertaking, only a few
months later, a journey which he must have dreaded because of the
hardships which he had already encountered on it—a journey which
led up to an altitude of 18,000 feet, and could only be accomplished
by a mountaineer in vigorous health. To face that journey was clearly
to risk life itself. And yet he took that risk.

During that autumn of 1928 he had a talk with Lala Khub Ram,
who was one of his oldest friends. The boys of the school had been

---

*   Acts 20:22-5.

acting a play in which the hero, King Ramchandra, praises the married life. After the play was over, Khub Ram got one of the actors to recite the speech of Rama concerning marriage, and then said with great earnestness: "Sadhuji, you ought to get married for the sake of your own health and comfort. In that way you will get some rest."

Sundar Singh answered with equal earnestness: "My only rest, Lalaji, is in the grave."

This story was told me by Chand Mal, who heard it. There is no doubt in my mind that Sundar Singh meant just what he said. He was clearly looking forward to an early death.

We know how martyrdom and death for the sake of religion is in the blood of the Sikhs as a religious people. We know also how Sundar Singh carried over this ideal, along with his eagerness to practice it, into his new life as a Christian. He had set his whole mind upon a literal following of our Lord, and was disappointed when his own life lingered on in a somewhat aimless manner after he had passed the age when Christ Himself suffered on the Cross. We have seen, further, how his mind dwelt constantly upon the triumphs and sufferings of the martyrs in every age of the Church.

When, therefore, his own health became so impaired that it seemed no longer possible to accomplish his previous journeys into Tibet, he seems to have felt the urgent call within to go out at any cost and look death in the face, whether it should come on the road, or in the Forbidden Land itself. His own life had often been threatened. It might be that one more venture of faith would bring to him the martyrdom he so long desired.

Therefore—so it appears—when he set out from Sabathu on that journey in April, 1929, he had already counted the cost. He would seek to share the baptism wherewith Christ had been baptized, and to drink the cup which He had drunk. Deep down in his heart was the thought—almost the hope—that he would meet his death on this last journey.

Such a premonition would account for his exact instructions about the fulfilment of the simple provisions of his will, wherein he left everything for the encouragement of the Christian education of young children, and for the furtherance of mission work in Tibet. Just as he had expected death on his previous journey in 1927, and had quoted to his friends the verses from the Acts of the Apostles,* so he looked forward to death again in 1929. He felt sure that afflictions awaited him, and anticipated that those who loved him should "see his face no more." He went "bound in the spirit" unto that "Jerusalem" which he was seeking with such earnestness in Tibet.

There is a letter written by the Rev. T. E. Riddle to Mr. Popley, dated May 23rd, 1930, which contains these words: "People imagine that the Sadhu wanted to be in solitude. He never wanted that: and the 'hermit' idea never appealed to him. Sabathu gave him all the solitude he needed."

Though this very brief statement hardly takes full account of his longing for a far deeper quiet and retirement than his home at Sabathu could afford, Mr. Riddle is undoubtedly right in saying that the "hermit" idea never appealed to Sundar Singh. He sought to *suffer* for Christ's sake rather than to spend the rest of his life as a hermit.

Somewhere on the road into Tibet he seems to have met his end. To those who have travelled up and down these mountain tracks of the Himalayas, with all their loneliness—far away from any human habitation—it is possible to picture what may have happened. There are mountain slopes where the track runs, like a narrow ledge, with a precipitous descent of thousands of feet beneath, and high rocks overhead. Even to look down often makes the head dizzy, the distance below is so great. To Sundar Singh, with his eyesight already greatly impaired, a sudden giddiness may have come, due to heart failure, and his sure foot may have faltered. Those who were in the caravan may have been far ahead, knowing nothing of what was happening behind. In the state of his chronic heart trouble, such a journey, if unaccompanied by any friend and helper, had every chance of being fatal. The slip of a foot, when no one was near, and a fall down the

---

* Acts 20:24-5

mountain-side might have occurred. If, when darkness came on, no trace of him was to be found, very little search would be made. The caravan would pass on.

Even, as Mr. Riddle suggests, this later stage of the road may not have been reached. Heart-failure or haemorrhage may have come to him lower down on the Pilgrim Road, or an attack of cholera which proves fatal in a few hours. If he were in the midst of the crowd at that time, no record would have been left of his death, and his dead body would be thrown into the sacred River Ganges. While, therefore, it seems to us strange that not a single word about him has ever reached us from any source all these years, it is not altogether unaccountable. Others have vanished out of sight, in a crowded country like India, by a similar fate.

If, on the other hand, we turn again to the second alternative for a moment and regard him as still living in retirement, then it is hard to think, with one so considerate as Sundar Singh, that he would not have sent long ago some message to his friends. He had promised Mr. Watson that he would do so if he were ill. He wrote in the same strain to Mrs. Parker, whom he loved with deep filial affection.

He would surely have fulfilled his promise if he had been alive, for he would have realized that thousands were mourning his death. He was not the type of person to be indifferent to human sorrow. He loved his friends too well.

No! The conclusion seems very nearly certain that he gave up his life in the service of his Master, sometime in the year 1929, probably in the month of May or June, while seeking to reach Tibet. "Through much tribulation" he had entered at last into the Kingdom. While no one among the thousands of his friends was at his side when death came, the Lord stood by him. The Good Shepherd led him through the valley. His rod and staff comforted him.

Chapter XV

His Living Message

WHAT a wonderful life the Sadhu lived! More than anything else, perhaps, the true greatness of his personality may be judged by the unquenchable belief held by so many people, both in India and Europe, that he has not even yet met his death. For this conviction still lingers on, year after year, in the hearts of those who loved and revered him. They have not been able, even after more than five years have passed by, to think of him as dead. Though I cannot now share their belief, I can well understand the sentiment that lies behind it.

When the time comes at last to estimate, at its full value, all that Sundar Singh has accomplished, both in his own country and in the West, the highest place is likely to be given to his singular influence in bringing those who met him, or heard him speak, back to the living Christ as their personal Lord and Master. Wherever I have gone, in distant lands across the sea, there have been earnest men and women who have told me, with heart-felt conviction, that the Sadhu had brought into their lives a new devotion to their Saviour and a new assurance of moral victory through His grace. Their former experience of constant inner defeat had been changed to a joyous sense of freedom, and they have been able to utter, along with the apostle, the song of triumph: "In all these things we are more than conquerers through him who loved us." For they have learnt, through the Sadhu's example, to realize afresh that love of Christ, as a burning passion, constraining them to sacrifice and service. Since then, they have been able to live as Christians, on an altogether different plane.

One of these earnest and devoted souls, Mary Simpson, a nurse of St. Catherine's Hospital, Cawnpore, from 1921-1927, has given me permission to quote freely from her home letters wherever Sundar Singh is mentioned. Her simple story, told to her sister without any thought of publication, gives a remarkably vivid picture of the exceeding beauty of that devotion to his Lord and Saviour, which the Sadhu was able to bring home to the hearts of others. Fire kindles fire; and in these letters we can feel the glow of Christ's love, which burnt with a bright flame within his own heart, as he lived and moved among men.

"He has the same calm and happy face," she writes to her sister. "It is calm, and yet so intensely full of life. As he spoke about Christ revealing God's love to sinful men, his voice softened, his face changed, his eyes glowed and his whole countenance was lighted up with brightness. It was not so much his sermon—nothing could have been simpler than that; it was rather the Sadhu himself who attracted us as he brought Christ's living presence with him. Whenever I look at him, as he speaks from the pulpit, I never have the least difficulty in knowing that he has seen Christ. My difficulty is to believe all the time, that it is not Christ Himself who is speaking to us. What the Psalm says, 'When I wake up after Thy likeness,' is literally true of him.

"The Church was packed to the doors: people were sitting on the floor and on the pulpit steps: every bit of the floor space was occupied. After the service was over, they all crowded round him and I was able to look on. They love him so much, because he is one of themselves, an Indian, and also because of his greatness and goodness.

"He is so absolutely courteous to everyone, young and old alike, dirty and ragged and poor. Everyone is the same to him. One very old man, with a stick under his arm, went up to him and fell at his feet. I could not hear all that they said, but the Sadhu was so tender to him and lifted him up. The old man's tears were streaming down his face. I think that he wanted to give the Sadhu his stick, but I did not know the reason why.

"It was the Sadhu's tenderness and gentleness that struck me most of all. I hardly know how to tell you all about him. It sounds so ordinary and commonplace, and yet it was extraordinary in every way. I could not follow all his sermon in Urdu, because he speaks so quickly and every now and then turns away his head while he is speaking. But I got the drift of it all, which was the Love of Christ."

On another occasion, Miss Simpson met him at Kotgarh, where again he preached about Christ and His constraining love. The Christians came from long distances to hear him, and there were those who were not Christians also present. He took as his text the words—"Hitherto ye have asked nothing in My name. Ask and ye shall receive, that your joy may be full." His message seemed to come straight from Christ Himself and to give to her just what she needed most. He made those present realize that everything was possible through prayer and added one of his own striking illustrations. Just as there must first be fire, if the smoke is to ascend heavenwards, even so the fire of the Holy Spirit must bum in our hearts, if our prayers are to rise like the smoke out of the fire. For prevailing prayer ascends right up to the heart of God. Then he spoke about the visions that Christ gives to His own followers—inner visions that are so bright and glorious that no amount of persecution can take away the joy and peace which comes when Christ is thus present in the inmost heart.

"The whole force of his preaching," she writes, "seems to rest in the one strong conviction of Christ's love, which is the burden of his message. He is one who *knows:* one who *sees* Christ face to face. That quiet little church at Kotgarh, in the middle of the mountains, had no grandeur about it. It was all so poverty-stricken; and yet I felt truly that Christ was present there in their midst. I did not wish to speak to the Sadhu afterwards. Like every true prophet, the virtue goes out of him when he is giving a message. And I had received the message—that was all I needed. Now, after seeing and hearing him, I know that everything is possible. To-day I have seen what man can become like if he truly lives in Christ. For the Sadhu is very like Christ—even his face shows it; and his presence sheds it round about him, wherever he goes. It has indeed been wonderful to have met him."

These last words have been uppermost in my own mind while I have been writing. For it has, indeed, been "wonderful to have met him," and the inner life has been enriched thereby. The constant remembrance of him, during all these intervening years, has brought me nearer to Christ. When I was with him in the Himalayas and at Delhi, as this memoir will show, he strengthened my own faith and helped me to keep the pure flame of Christ's love burning bright. Therefore, it has been my one great longing that the reading of this book may be the means of passing on to others that same devotion to Christ. Especially, I have longed that this may happen among those who are still young in the faith and perplexed by the difficulties of the modern world. To them it must bring a wonderful assurance to know, through his example, that the power of Christ's love can be manifested to-day, in circumstances so different and in lands so remote, with the same victory over human sin and weakness. How can they possibly doubt the power of that transcendent love, when they see it in Sadhu Sundar Singh? Surely a love that can achieve, in the strangest surroundings, such miracles of grace, can overcome their own weakness and make them strong in their turn. Let my own testimony of a lifetime, be added to theirs. For Sundar's personal friendship has made me strong, when otherwise I might have been weak in the faith.

Not only does the Sadhu's life carry with it a personal message to meet our own individual needs, thus encouraging and cheering us on; it has also a message for the whole Church, both in the West and in the East.

Here in the West, where this memoir is being written, his life seems to tell us to get rid of our narrow divisions and our false racial pride; to break down the hard barriers between one race and another, so that we may all become one Man in Christ Jesus. And to the East, the Sadhu brings the message that Christ belongs to them no less than to the West; that it is their function to express Him truly as belonging to the East. It is theirs to offer to the West a new vision of Christ as He walks the Eastern road and dwells among the Eastern village folk in lowly poverty, simplicity and self-denial. Above all, it is theirs to renew in the whole of Christendom that "first love" of Christ, with all its ardour of personal devotion, which shall uplift and transform mankind.

Notes

The Franciscans in Tibet [p. 5]

It is difficult for us to realize the amazing courage of those early Franciscans and the vast, imminent threat to Christian civilization in the West by the Mongols which was partly averted by their daring action. In a book called *The Challenge of Central Asia**–the following passage occurs:

"In the year 1238, Europe was suddenly awakened to the Mongol danger. Panic seized the minds of men as they heard of these savage hordes who had 'brought terrible devastation to the eastern parts (of Europe), laying them waste with carnage.' A curious little incident which has been preserved shows how widespread was the fear inspired by the Mongol invasion. In the year 1240, the people of Gothland and Friesland did not dare to go to Yarmouth for the herring fishery as usual, in consequence of which it is recorded that 'the herrings were so cheap that forty or fifty sold for a piece of silver.'

"It was at this time, when 'distress and darkness and the gloom of anguish' were brooding over Europe, that the Christian Church rose up declaring that in one way only could civilization be saved from doom: by winning the barbarians for Christ, and through Christianity to civilization.

* World Dominion Press, London

"Inspired by these motives the first Franciscan missionaries set out on their adventurous journey to Asia. Three names stand out among those who embarked on this courageous campaign: Friar John de Plano Carpini, Friar William of Rubruck, and somewhat later, Friar Odoric.

"Carpini set out from Lyons on Easter Day, 1245, on the first important journey made by a European into the vast Mongol Empire. The expedition occupied two years and involved great hardships. Carpini and his companions often slept on the bare snow, and they suffered much from hunger. Carpini brought back a letter from Kuyuk Khan (grandson of Genghiz Khan) to the Pope, which ends by asking the Pope to come to the East and do homage to the Mongol rulers: 'And if you do not observe the order of God... then we will know you as our enemy.' Carpini did not live long after his return to Europe. Worn out by the hardships he had endured, he died in 1252.

"William of Rubruck left Europe for the East the year after Carpini's death. He was sent by King Louis IX of France, who gave him a little money for his journey, letters to the Mongol Khan and a Bible. The story of his journey is vivid and accurate and a valuable record of travel. Rubruck returned to Europe in 1255. The results of his mission were somewhat doubtful, as the Mongol Khan had no real desire to receive the Christian message. Rubruck's references to the 'Christians' he met in Central Asia are interesting; he was often shocked by their ignorance and disgusted by their paganism; of one group he says: 'They were ignorant of all things regarding the Christian religion, excepting only the name of Christ.'

"Friar Odoric set out for the East about 1318. After a long and hazardous journey by way of India he returned overland through Tibet, Persia, and the land of the famous Assassins. He died in Italy in 1331. Soon after his death his fame both as saint and traveller spread far and wide."

Christ's Universal Gospel [p. 28]

IN THE Gospel story we find an ever-deepening sympathy, both in word and deed, with the devout and humble men and women of other faiths, who were born outside the Jewish Community. This was developed still further in the story of the Acts of the Apostles, which follows directly after the Gospels. It comes to its complete expression in the great words of St. Paul: "In him there can be neither Jew nor Greek, Barbarian, Scythian, bond nor free, but all are one Man in Christ Jesus."

The narrowness of the religious patriotism of the Hebrew Church, which regarded itself alone as the Chosen People of God, and crudely marked off everyone who was not a Jew by the name of Gentile, was continually challenged by our Lord both in word and action. Coming as He did from the narrow surroundings of an obscure Jewish country town in Galilee, He at once put on one side the conventional barriers which separated one man from another. Quite early in His ministry He proclaimed among His own townsmen in Nazareth a larger and ampler faith in God's fatherly love for all mankind. By commending Naaman the Syrian and the Gentile widow of Sarepta as more acceptable to God than the chosen people of the Jewish race, He so incurred their wrath that they "rose up and thrust him out of the city, and led him unto the brow of the hill, whereon their city was built, that they might cast him down headlong."

Thus from the very first Jesus freely proclaimed His Gospel of God's love, at whatever cost to His own life. In a similar manner, He commended in glowing words the faith of the Roman Centurion and of the Syro-Phoenician woman. In the old Jewish Scriptures the Hebrew word "neighbour" was constantly used merely of a Hebrew compatriot. Indeed, in the Law of Moses, that was its common significance. But when the Scribe asked Jesus the question: "Who, then, is my neighbour?" He enlarged the meaning of the word out of all recognition and gave it a universal moral value. He set forward the Samaritan, whom the Jews hated, as the true neighbour, because he fulfilled God's great commandment of love. The Jewish priest and Levite, who passed by on the other side, were condemned by Jesus because they had not fulfilled this commandment. Such teaching as this was revolutionary both in Judea and in Galilee. It is only because we have got used to the new significance of the word "neighbour," which Jesus gave it, that we do not realize what a revolution it implies.

The disciples, who showed to the full the class prejudices and narrow patriotisms of their age, wished to call down fire from heaven ("even as Elias did") and destroy a Samaritan village, which did not receive Jesus. But He rebuked them strongly, saying: "Ye know not what manner of spirit ye are of. For the Son of Man is come, not to destroy men's lives, but to save them."

This whole attitude of Jesus to man as man was fundamental with Him, because His life was built up on one great central principle. He declared that in every condition of human existence God is "Our Father." The Heavenly Father loves each one of His children with an individual and personal love. The farther away the child has wandered, the more passionately the Father's heart goes out in love for him. He eagerly follows with His forgiveness even the prodigal son who has almost forgotten Him. As the prodigal comes home, the Father runs to meet him and lavishes His forgiveness upon him from the depth of His loving heart.

Such a Heavenly Father, loving even His enemies, could obviously have no favorites. All His children were equally dear to Him. His love was like the sunshine and the gracious rain. It descended on all sides. This universality of God's love made it perfect; and we ourselves were to love in the same perfect manner. "Be ye perfect," said Jesus, "even as your Heavenly Father is perfect."

As the unique Son of that Heavenly Father, Jesus came to reveal perfectly on earth His character. The love of Jesus was of the same quality as the Father's love. He would not "break a bruised reed" or "quench a smoking flax," but would rather "bind up the broken-hearted and set at liberty them that were bruised." All the strivings of humanity, age after age, to find God—however broken and imperfect they might be—He would take into His own healing hands and bless. He came among men to seek and to save that which was lost.

Sundar Singh himself, as a Christian, never wavered for a moment in his conviction that the religious background of his early life, as a Sikh, which he had inherited from his father and mother, was essentially good and not evil. It needed the transforming touch of Christ to complete it, and the power of His risen life to endow it with new strength. But it must not be cast aside and rejected.

He believed, that is to say, that the long search for God down all the ages, and especially in his own country, had been a noble search with the blessing of God behind it. He was proud of all those saintly men and women who had maintained and carried on this unending search—never shrinking back from the cost, however great it might be, if only they might find the Truth.

Yoga and Prayer [p. 30]

Certain appropriate methods of controlling the body and mind, in order to create an atmosphere of stillness, have been practiced by deeply religious men and women in India from earliest times. These are called "Yoga," or Union, and one who practices them is called "Yogi." It is quite possible that the Indian temperament is peculiarly adapted for these special methods, and therefore they have been continued for countless generations. They are undertaken as a preparation towards the inner communion between the spirit of man and the Divine Spirit, and the words of the Psalm: "Be still and know that I am God," are in very close keeping with Indian religious thought.

One who had practiced Yoga for nearly a whole lifetime with this intention in view, described to me the aim which he had before him. "The body and mind," he said, "have to be brought into perfect harmony and repose, so that they may receive, without any interruption, the inflow of that Divine Life which pervades the universe."

There are well-known dangers which have to be avoided if anyone for religious purposes seriously engages in Yoga. Self-hypnotism may result instead of God-realization. Or again, mere quietism may lead on to selfish aloofness from the stern hardships of life, which have to be bravely faced if man's will is to be made strong. Men of religion in India have been fully alive to dangers of this kind, and yet they have never discountenanced on this account the practice of Yoga.

In the Indian Church hitherto, there has been an instinctive and natural reaction against the use of Yoga in Christian circles. Missionaries from the very beginning have often spoken against it, and there are clearly good reasons why they should do so when dealing with an infant community. But in recent years there have been a few sincere and earnest adventurers in Christian living who have sought through their own spiritual experience to relate this agelong Indian practice of Yoga to the transforming touch of Christ. In this connection they uphold the principle which Christ Himself declared when He said: "Think not that I am come to destroy the law or the prophets: I am not come to destroy, but to fulfil." (Matthew 5:17)

Those who are seeking to recover its practice in the Indian Church, feel that Yoga may be a help towards overcoming the difficulties by which East and West alike are now confronted, owing to the strain and stress of modem life. They seek Christ's living presence through an atmosphere of rest and repose. And they remember, while practicing Yoga, the words of the Saviour: "Come unto me, all ye that labour and are heavy laden, and I will give you rest." (Matthew 11:28) One writer has pointed out a somewhat doubtful etymology between the word "Yoga" and the English word "yoke."

Sadhu Sundar Singh had already learnt certain forms of Yoga from a devout Hindu Sannyasin. Although he found these practices unsatisfying when he became a Christian, he did not abandon them altogether, but rather sought to transform them and use them in Christ's service. He kept long hours of silent waiting for the Divine Spirit to flow into his own life and quicken his inner being. His whole conception of prayer was influenced by this thought of stillness in order to receive the divine message.

Perhaps the best method of explaining briefly what certain leading Indian Christians have been seeking, by reviving Yoga in a Christian form, is to quote somewhat fully from the pamphlet published by Mr. A. S. Appasamy in Madras, which deals with this difficult subject.*

"Communion with God," he writes, "is not a matter of reading or knowledge, but rather of practice. It is not so much a science as an art. It was not possible for me to come in contact with Western mystics who were practicing that art. But I found that there were sages in India who, according to their lights, were practicing Yoga, or union with God, and who had indeed attained a high degree of proficiency in it. I did not hesitate to learn from them, when I found I could not learn the practice of communion with God from any Christian mystic that I knew in India."

The writer describes, with some detail, two special modes of Yoga practiced in ancient India, and explains how in his own Christian life he has been able to make use of them with great benefit. He has found out by practical experience that they have strengthened and confirmed his faith in Christ and made prayer more real and effectual.

"All medical authorities," he adds, "are agreed in regarding worry, care and anxiety as factors that sap the energy and destroy life. Now, in our contemplation (i.e. through Yoga), we are wonderfully delivered from these life-destroying agencies. Peace, joy and quiet reign in our souls and these build up body and soul, just as their opposites destroy them."

"Reason," he writes again, "is a God-given gift and should be fully exercised. When difficult problems arise, we should endeavor to reason and come to a conclusion.... But when we reach the point where we find ourselves helpless, then we may resort to the prayer of contemplation. In contemplation (i.e. Yoga) reason ceases to function, but problems solve themselves naturally; the decision we are unable to

---

* Yoga and Prayer, by Dewan Bahadur A. S. Appasamy. Published by Christian Literature Society of India, Madras, 1926.

reach, in the normal human way, by processes of thought becomes quite clear to us."

Again, he writes: "The practice of ineffable communion with Christ in contemplative prayer (Yoga) tends to reduce to its minimum the element of petition in prayer. We are inclined to ask for less and less as we grow in the life of contemplation.... The different parts of the personality are completely brought under the sway of God and we begin to love Him wholly. All the different elements in our being are summoned and devoted in worship and reverence and love to the living Christ."

What I have witnessed in India has gone far to confirm the impression, received long ago, that the East in these matters has much to teach the West in return for the things that the West has taught the East. Above all, it has become clear to me that the "shattered nerves" of the West, including my own, need healing; and while it is unfortunately true that the fever of modern life has already widely penetrated the East, yet it is also true that there are those who have been spiritually strong enough to resist this backward, eddying current of the age in which we life. These victorious spirits can tell us—if only we are wise and humble enough to listen—how we, too, many overcome our weakness and receive from Christ that inner peace which He is waiting to give us.

The essence of Yoga, as we have seen, is spiritual communion with the Unseen. Its method is that of self-surrender in quietude of spirit, relaxing the human effort while allowing the divine grace to inflow.

The writer I have quoted explains cogently that the fulfilment of the first commandment of love to God, "with all the heart, and with all the soul, and with all the mind, and with all the strength," cannot be fully accomplished unless these several parts of the one human personality are integrated and united. They must all act in unison together. He holds that one integrating factor, which may be used in effecting this desired end, is Yoga.

It is active, and yet passive. It demands human effort, and yet is entirely dependent on the divine will. Actively, the human will, with all its wayward impulses and baser passions, is surrendered. Passively, it waits for the divine inflow of new light and love.

In his own case—as he describes it in his pamphlet—the moment of change was reached when he saw with his inner mind a vision of Christ Himself. This vision remained with him, silently filling his whole being with inward peace, and it has now become with him a constant experience repeating itself in those moments when the mind is absolutely still. But he is very careful to add that this inner vision, which has come to himself, is only one mode of realization and perhaps not the most important. For God fulfils Himself in many ways to each humble man of heart, who makes the complete surrender of love to Him in the silence.

> "There are diversities of gifts, but the same Spirit.
> "And there are differences of administration, but the same Lord.
> "And there are diversities of operation, but it is the same God who worketh all in all."*

---

*   1 Corinthians 12:4-7

Bibliography

A. The Sadhu's own writings:

(1) *Visions of the Spiritual World.* Published by Macmillan.
[This contains a brief description of the spiritual life beyond the grave as seen by the Sadhu in visions.]

(2) *Reality and Religion.* Published by Macmillan.
[In this book the Sadhu has put down some ideas as illustrations concerning the love of God and the wonders of His creation, which were the outcome of his meditations.]

(3) *Meditations on Various Aspects of the Spiritual Life.* Published by Macmillan.
[This volume deals with certain of the difficulties of the spiritual life, such as the meaning of pain and suffering, of opposition and criticism. He meditates also upon the life in Christ, and the Kingdom of God.]

(4) *The Search after Reality.* Published by Macmillan.
[Here the Sadhu writes about the Eastern religions among which he had lived in closest contact. He shows how Christ's message brings each of them to its true fulfilment.]

(5) *With and Without Christ.* Published by Harper & Brothers.
[This was the last writing of the Sadhu. It was published by
Harpers in 1929. The book is composed of incidents taken
from the lives of Christians and non-Christians, which illustrate the difference of living with Christ and without Christ.
The last portion contains a remarkably vivid account of his
own Christian experience.]

(6) *At the Master's Feet.*
[This book of devotion has been published by Fleming H. Revell Company. In it the Master speaks to his disciple and explains
some of the questions that arise concerning the inner life.]

(7) *Par Christ et Pour Christ.*
[A translation into French of the addresses given by the Sadhu
in Switzerland. It is published by the Secretariat Suisse de la
Mission aux Indes, Lausanne.]

(8) *Soul-Stirring Messages.*
[Published at the C.M.S. Industrial Press, Sikandra, Agra. It
contains a series of the Sadhu's earlier addresses in India. The
translation is by Alfred Zahir, and it has been revised by the
Sadhu himself.]

B. The Sadhu's Life and Teaching:

Sadhu Sundar Singh, Called of God. By Mrs. Arthur Parker. Published by Fleming H. Revell Company.

The Message of Sadhu Sundar Singh. By Drs. Streeter and Appasamy.
Published by Macmillan.
[This book is a study of the Sadhu's religious experience from
the mystical standpoint.]

The Gospel of Sadhu Sundar Singh. By Dr. Heiler of Marburg. Published by George Allen and Unwin, London.

[This is the fullest account published in English and German of the Sadhu's life and teaching. The author replies, in a constructive manner, to the controversial attack made on the Sadhu's trust-worthiness by certain continental writers.]

Dia Legende Sundar Singhs. By O. Pfister. Published by P. Haupt, Berne, 1926.
[This book, written in German, deals with Sundar Singh's alleged miraculous experiences from the psychopathic standpoint. It rejects them as due to hallucination.]

Sundar Singh: The Lion-Hearted Warrior. By E. Sanders and Ethelred Judah. Published by Macmillan.

Scripture Testimony Index

The sheep know and hear His voice
John 10:3-4 · John 10:16

Matthew 10:19-20 · Acts 8:29 · Acts 13:2 · Acts 15:28 · Acts
16:6-10 · Acts 20:22 · Romans 8:14

While praying one night, Sadhu Sundar Singh felt impressed to
go to "someone from the valley below who was needing his immediate help." He left in the middle of the night—despite the
protestations of his friends—to go help this person. It was a few
days before he was back, and his friends learned of how he had
brought sorely needed assistance to the very person the Spirit had
summoned him to help!

Matthew 9:36 · Matthew 14:13-21 · Mark 1:41 · Mark 6:34 ·
Luke 7:13

When Sundar Singh visited the Lepers' Home at Chandkuri, he
spoke to them of the love of God and demonstrated that love by

taking the time to speak and bring comfort to each of the sick there. He left them with the comforting prayer of the Apostle Paul; asking that God's peace remain with them.

The void created by the loss of his mother, whom he dearly loved, pushed Sundar Singh to rebel against God. Soon he became the ringleader of a group of youths who attacked preaching missionaries. Ultimately, his anger resulted in him publicly burning the Christian scriptures.

Seeking resolution for the pain of his great personal loss—for which he blamed God—fifteen-year-old Sundar Singh had publicly burned the Gospels. But the act only increased his angst. After a great existential crisis, in which he agonized in prayer, Jesus appeared to the youth in a vision. Much like the Apostle Paul, Sundar Singh immediately went from being a persecutor to a believer, devoting his life to being an uncompromising disciple of Jesus Christ.

When Sadhu Sundar Singh was questioned about his having seen the Lord Jesus—whether the vision was objective or subjective—he would point to the fact that the experience completely and permanently changed him. The ultimate proof of this was shown in his fruitful life of joy and gladness even when facing suffering, hardship, persecution, and even death.

When all entreaties failed to persuade Sundar Singh to abandon his Christian faith or at least to keep it secret, he was driven from home and excommunicated from the Sikh religion. But young Sundar Singh writes about the peace that filled his heart even as he passed the first night outside in the cold under a tree. God's presence was with him.

Do not retaliate, instead behave honorably
Romans 12:17

Matthew 5:44

Some of the other theological students felt judged by Sundar's radical lifestyle and resented him for it. The ringleader of his student tormentors one day overheard Sundar tearfully praying for him. This broke the hard heart of this very student, which led to repentance and lifelong friendship.

Matthew 10:5-15 ·
Luke 9:1-6 · Luke 10:1-20

Partly because he had been thrust out of his father's house, and partly because his mother had always exalted the ascetic life of a Sadhu—or holy man—Sundar Singh chose a lifestyle that literally embodied Christ's sending out of the disciples with "nor purse, nor scrip."

Acts 5:41

Samuel Stokes writes about the Sadhu, who when he was just a boy, suffered terribly for his Master. One day, as they traveled through mountains, Sundar Singh was nearly overcome with illness. When Stokes asked him how he felt, Sundar's answer was, "I am very happy: how sweet it is to suffer for His sake!"

Sundar Singh was a great influence on his fellow students, inspiring them to abandon themselves to Christ's service. One student, like the Good Samaritan of the parable, carried a sick man on his back for miles to get care for him.

When Sadhu Sundar Singh was leaving Kiwar to go preach in the surrounding Tibetan villages, he was warned about thieves and robbers and was urged to go with a sword or a gun. But for the Sadhu, the Word of God was his sword, and he trusted God to protect him.

For Sundar Singh, following daily in the footsteps of Jesus was the one overriding desire of his life. To achieve this, he made the Urdu New Testament his one inseparable companion and studied it to such a degree that "it lived in his memory and fashioned his daily thoughts."

Sadhu Sundar Singh was remarkably observant, like His Savior, and employed parables and vivid illustrations to drive home his teachings about the great love of Jesus and the Holy Spirit.

When on a journey to Palestine, Sundar Singh drank water from a well and felt refreshed. But it was not long before he became thirsty again. This experience made him grateful for the fountain of Living Waters from which he had been privileged to drink since he surrendered his life to Jesus.

As we serve Him, the Lord will be our defense 96
Luke 10:19 · 2 Thessalonians 3:1-3

One beautiful starlit night, Sundar Singh was outside the house, looking down into the deep valley. His friend Shoran Singha saw him from a window, and then stood speechless as he watched a leopard approaching. But Sundar Singh turned toward the animal and held out his hand. The leopard laid down and offered his head to be stroked, as though he were a dog. Later the Sadhu said that he had no cause to tremble because he trusts in Christ.

Jesus will never send away those who come to Him
John 6:37

Father forgive them, for they know not what they do 117
Luke 23:34 · Acts 7:60

While Mr. Ishii was a free man, he lived recklessly, and became more and more hardened the more he was urged to repent. Eventually his ways led him to prison where he found the Savior. Now writing from prison, he was thankful to have found forgiveness and a new life of joy and contentment from God, even in the midst of suffering. Mr. Ishii's autobiography was one of the most heavily annotated books in Sundar Singh's library.

True disciples love Jesus more than even their own lives
Matthew 8:18-22 · Matthew 16:21-28 · Luke 9:57-62 · Luke 14:25-35

The fulness of God's joy comes through obedience 121
John 15:11 · Galatians 5:22 · Philippians 4:4 · Hebrews 12:2

Rev. T. E. Riddle, who translated Sadhu Sundar Singh's books, writes about the Sadhu's many struggles with health problems. Riddle observed of Sundar Singh that, "In hours of specially intense spiritual stress, when suffering deprivation for Christ's sake, the joy that came to him used to wipe away all the pain. He would explain that it was not joy in suffering, but that the pain itself was transmuted into joy."

Walking Together Press is a non-profit publishing company devoted to supporting grassroots libraries in Africa through global book sales and through providing free library editions.

To read our story, to see our catalog, and to learn more about how you can help us in our mission, visit our website at:

https://walkingtogether.press

www.ingramcontent.com/pod-product-compliance
Lightning Source LLC
Chambersburg PA
CBHW030222140626
46545CB00012B/2960